CHRIST'S BODY
IN
CORINTH

PAUL IN CRITICAL CONTEXTS

*The Paul in Critical Contexts series offers cutting-edge reexaminations
of Paul through the lenses of power, gender, and ideology.*

CHRIST'S BODY

IN

CORINTH

THE POLITICS OF A METAPHOR

YUNG SUK KIM

Fortress Press
Minneapolis

Cover design: Laurie Ingram
Cover image: View of the courtyard. Archaeological Museum, Corinth, Greece. Photo
    © Vanni / Art Resource, NY
Book design and typesetting: The HK Scriptorium, Inc.

Images are taken from *The Cities of Paul* © 2004 The President and Fellows of Harvard College.

Library of Congress Cataloging-in-Publication Data

Kim, Yung Suk.
  Christ's body in Corinth : the politics of a metaphor / Yung Suk Kim.
      p.   cm.
  Includes bibliographical references and index.
  ISBN 978-0-8006-6285-1 (alk. paper)
  1. Church—Biblical teaching. 2. Jesus Christ—Mystical body—History of doctrines—
Early church, ca. 30-600. 3. Bible. N.T. Corinthians, 1st—Criticism, interpretation, etc.
I. Title.

  BS2675.6.C5K56 2008
  227'.2064—dc22

                                                                      2008011512

The paper used in this publication meets the minimum requirements of American National Standard for Information Sciences—Permanence of Paper for Printed Library Materials, ANSI Z329.48-1984.

Manufactured in the U.S.A.

10 09 08   2 3 4 5 6 7 8 9 10

Contents

Acknowledgments

This book would not have seen the light if not for many persons who have supported my work, both professionally and personally. I give sincere, special thanks to my doctoral dissertation advisor, Professor Daniel M. Patte (Vanderbilt University), who took pains to read, guide, and encourage my work with critical comments; from beginning to end, never saying "no" but always "yes" to my academic interests. I also give my warmest thanks to Professor Fernando F. Segovia and all the members of my dissertation committee—Douglas Knight, Victor Anderson, and Kathy Gaca—who guided my research with patience and wisdom. I also give my deepest thanks to Professor Laurence Welborn at Fordham University for his encouragement and critical guidance in my research of Pauline theology and the Greco-Roman world. I also thank Professor Robert Brawley, my first seminary New Testament teacher at McCormick Theological Seminary, who read the full manuscript with some tangibly critical comments. I also want to acknowledge my dean, John Kinney at Samuel Dewitt Proctor School of Theology of Virginia Union University, and my colleagues for their support and understanding of my teaching and research. I also give my heartfelt thanks to Rob Worley, my friend and mentor, who gives me care and courage when I am in need. I also would like to express my special thanks for the community of McCormick Theological Seminary that has sustained my studies in a healthy way. I regret that I cannot add all of the people to whom I should express my deepest thanks.

I cannot find proper words to express special thanks to my family— a resting place for the soul. My wife Yong-Jeong's loving sacrifice and my daughters' (HyeRim, HyeKyung, and HyeIn) vast patience with my work will never be forgotten. Finally, I also give my special thanks to Dr. Neil Elliott, my editor at Fortress Press, who recognized the value of this book and helped to shape it into a readable work for the wider public.

INTRODUCTION

The Price of Unity

"Now you are the body of Christ and individually members of it." (1 Cor 12:27)

Many scholars have read Paul's metaphor *sōma christou*—the "body of Christ"[1]—as a metaphor for the church as an organism,[2] ideally characterized by a unity that overcomes the problems raised by diversity.[3] For instance, Margaret Mitchell reads 1 Corinthians as a deliberative rhetoric in which the "body of Christ" becomes a central metaphor for an organic unity.[4] Other scholars have read the phrase primarily in connection with Paul's theology, however, as a metaphor related to ethical exhortation and/or mission.[5] I argue that approaching this language as a metaphor for ecclesiological organism alone overlooks an ethical meaning that Paul wants to evoke by speaking of the "body of Christ." Further, what I will call this "ecclesial-organic" approach sometimes condones, or understands Paul as advocating, a dominant ideology of hierarchical unity, an ideology promoted by the Greco-Roman rhetoric of *homonoia* (concord).

Various problems arise—in popular Christianity as well as in scholarship—from this understanding of *sōma christou* as ecclesiological organism. First, the metaphor *body of Christ* comes to function as a mark of an exclusive boundary that silences the voice of marginality in the community and society. Second, by limiting the notion of the "body of Christ" to language concerning "belonging," this approach leads to and supports a narrow, rigid, and closed conception of the community. Third, and consequently, this approach tends to prevent the possibility of an ethical interpretation of the "body of Christ" in the community and in the larger context of society—especially in the context of power conflicts both inside and outside the community.

1

Interpreting the "body of Christ" as an ecclesiological organism is plausible: Paul does employ such an organism metaphor in the sense of unity. But we should not stop here. There are other possibilities that we should not ignore. In fact, understanding the Pauline "body of Christ" requires a multifaceted approach that asks a series of questions:

1. How should we conceive community?
2. How should we understand the function of boundary between the community and outside?
3. What does it mean to be a "member of Christ"?
4. How should we understand the "body of Christ" in the context of the situation that Paul addresses in Corinth?

For example, if we regard the progression from 1 Cor 1:1-9 ("called as apostle of Christ and called as partners of Christ") to 1:10-17 ("united *in the gospel of the cross of Christ* and its power"), we can see that for Paul, "being united in the same mind and for the same purpose" (1:10) is not a matter simply of belonging to a single ecclesiological body, but is rather a matter of having a mind and purpose framed by the same gospel that does not empty the cross of Christ of its power (1:17). Furthermore, we shall see that, as these verses also show, the Corinthians should not say either "I belong to Paul" or "I belong to Apollos" or "I belong to Cephas" or "I belong to Christ" (1:12), because being in Christ Jesus does not mean "belonging to a party"; rather, it means being associated with "the cross of Christ," which should not be emptied of its power.

The "Body of Christ" Today

One of my greatest concerns in these pages is the tendency, within both Christianity and biblical studies, to claim Christ as a boundary-marker—an arrogant and exclusivist claim. Many times in history, such an exclusivist posture (in the name of the church as the body of Christ) has caused great evil, such as the Crusades, the Holocaust, various wars, and the evils of racism, sexism, homophobia, and classism. Imagined "others" are treated as no-bodies, and as targets of the types of Christian mission fueled by a particular way of imagining universalism. Unfortunately, a prevalent reading of *sōma christou* (body of Christ) in 1 Corinthians as a metaphor for the group as an institutional or ecclesial organism contributes to this exclusivism by seeking to unify the community that is the church at the price of diversity, while marginalizing others and their vision of the community. Such unity-oriented language is a double-edged sword, destructive both within the community and in its relationships with other people.[6] In the community, such language repudiates differences and diversity.[7] It also separates the church from the world by functioning as a boundary marker. By contrast, understanding the "body of Christ" as a metaphor for those associated with the crucified one allows for identifying that body with many broken human bodies and communities through history and culture. That this reading of 1 Corinthians has emerged only rarely may be due to our preoccupation with "belonging," a concern that leads to a kind of sectarian mentality that ultimately caused many conflicts in Paul's time, and in ours today as well, as seen, for example, in modern episodes of ethnic cleansing or in the Israeli-Palestinian conflict. Today, as I witness all kinds of sectarian movements around the world, I cry: Where is there hope? Is there no other way to conceive of the "body of Christ" in the world?

My thesis regarding the metaphor of the "body of Christ" shifts the focus from unity to diversity. I share Jacques Derrida's problems with the language of unity:[8] Who gets to speak about unity?[9] Is unity an essential goal? Or is it an ideologically disguised political rhetoric of control? Did Paul really emphasize unity as we conceive of it today? Did Paul adopt the metaphorical sense of the body as an institutional organism, as used by the Stoics? I will argue that 1 Corinthians offers and supports a very different understanding of "body of Christ." Instead of a static, objective metaphorical understanding of body representing boundary, I will argue for a conception of the "body of Christ" as a dynamic metaphor, as a "living body."

This alternative interpretation is crucial today because we must recognize diversity and differences with respectful disagreement and "soft" borders. Indeed, from the perspective of the powerless or the marginalized, unity often is not the solution to their predicaments, because it too often serves a rhetoric of power that sacrifices diversity. Often in the context of centralized powers and movements like imperialism or neo-colonialism, diversity may be allowed insofar as it serves unity. As such, diversity is never truly weighed when we think, practice, and imagine the "body of Christ" as traditional ecclesiologies have projected it, by positing a static, objective view of the "body of Christ" as the church (1 Cor 12:27). Today, the traditional rhetoric of community based in objective unity is being challenged by voices from the margins that confront injustice and inequality in the community and in the world.

Paul's argument presupposes that the divisiveness of the Corinthian community results not from a lack of unity but from a failure on the part of its members to acknowledge and respect the diversity present in the community. Those members who maintain "hard" boundaries exemplify this problem ("I belong to Cephas" . . .) that results from a hierarchical construction of the body based on the idolatry of power, honor, and wealth. If this assessment of the divisiveness in the Corinthian community is shown to be plausible, reading 1 Corinthians as a discourse advocating unity actually compounds the problem rather than solving it. All interpretation that calls for unity without true diversity as the solution to the problem in Corinth cements the hierarchical power structure, which is the real source of the problem, and treats Paul's text as imposing rules and norms on the community. But unity is not the goal or purpose of Paul's letter because in Greco-Roman society, unity can be a destructive and oppressive language.

It is with this suspicion about unity that I turn to 1 Corinthians, a text that I and other Christians view as Scripture. In view of the world I describe below, an intentional reimagining of the "body of Christ" based on diversity is crucial. Thus, my study of Paul's letter will examine closely the ideological issues involved in the structures of authority and power within the community itself and between the Christian community and other communities. But I also will examine closely the ideological issues reflected by the scholarly interpretations of Paul's letters. What construction of authority and power is implied by modern studies that presume the ecclesial-organic understanding of "body of Christ"? Although I recognize, in light of the history of interpretation that this letter can be interpreted as a call to unity, I want to explore an alternative way of reading this metaphor and the letter. Paul presents a theological and ethical challenge to the Corinthians' narrow vision of community so that they will become the "body of Christ," understood as the *crucified* body of Christ.[10]

I will argue that Paul is doing something other than advocating unity in 1 Cor 12:27, as most scholars interpret it. From the perspective of one who has been and is marginalized by the traditional interpretation of unity, I must question that interpretation. Why does it ignore a more liberating reading of the text? Why does it prefer a reading that can support a hegemonic discourse on the part of colonialist or racist oppressors?

Reading as a Citizen of the World

Dramatically altering its course in the 1970s, biblical interpretation moved away from a Eurocentric, objective model of interpretation to one of liberation and postmodern deconstruction.[11] This shift begins with the recognition that readers employ a diversity of analytical approaches that coincide with their concerns for ethical responsibility.[12] Accordingly, biblical or theological studies, along with literary and cultural studies, have raised a new set of ethical and hermeneutical questions related to readers. For Paul Ricoeur, for example, these are important hermeneutical questions: "Who speaks? Who acts? Who tells a story? And who is the subject of moral imputation?"[13] Reading is a mutual process between the text and the reader. Neither dominates. As a reader of sacred text and context, I register my own voice expressing a marginal, deconstructive and reconstructive hermeneutic[14] in an effort to recover a diversified global community that has been fragmented.[15]

Inevitably, I am reading "myself" in the Bible (and in the world) along with the joyful challenge of reading "with others."[16] I am no longer interested in finding a single truth,[17] in the flat sense in which Pilate asks Jesus, "What is truth?" (John 18:38),[18] but am interested rather in the *diversity* of truths in our life today as the life-abundant truth to which Jesus came to bear witness (John 18:37). I read the Bible with "others," joining in the common struggle for meaningful, faithful existence in the midst of an unfaithful, hopeless world. In a way, my hermeneutical key is the others who constitute my—our—stories.[19] This kind of experiential, intrinsic connection to the world and the Bible creates space for conversation with the past (history, literature, interpretation) and a challenge to reimagine an alternative world that honors life and bodiliness, including mortality, as God's gift.[20] I intend to bear in mind both the world that I come from and the world for which I live. Interpreting as a reader in the world always involves our interpretation of where we are, who we are, and what we are doing.

The world we live in now is severely fragmented by religion, race, culture, gender, class, and the various ideologies that accompany them. We must analyze the rationales or ideologies behind such divisions of the community because divisions of the community affect all people. Here in the United States, for example, the struggles related to race, class, and culture are obvious and reemerge every day. A minority of people in each community busy themselves with keeping their own disproportionate share of the pie, to the detriment of the majority of people in their communities who are poor, third world immigrants, and strangers. People of the same culture flock together for worship and social cohesion and often remain in their comfort zones and build walls that exclude others. The poor and the unfortunate become estranged and hopelessly marginalized because the dominant conception of the community is too narrow to embrace them. The world situation may now be darker than in any time in history because of dividing and destructive ideologies. This deep and very real division is often hidden beneath the guise of multiculturalism or globalism, where people are told they are included but in fact, they have no choice but to yield to a harmful, global economic and political system. We must ask, then, who gets to define community, and how do specific definitions of community serve different interests?

In this world of hurt and fragmentation, I seek a world of redemption and the "redemption of our bodies" (Rom 8:23). I feel both hope and despair as I reflect on the recent history of my own country, Korea, formerly united but now torn apart by war and conflicting ideologies. Our people in the Diaspora today live out their destiny in many parts of the world, including the United States. We need redemptive healing through which many people can come together to celebrate their place in the world. My heart and mind cannot rest as I remember the then-young Korean men and women who were taken away from their homes in the last century to serve Japanese colonialism. Many have since died; others are still alive, with no hope of returning home. Some of us, including me, live away from home by choice in our quest for a better life. But living in the United States as a "border" person, I discover ambiguities in my identity and ask: Where do I belong? Can I say, like Diogenes the Cynic (404–323 BCE), "I am a citizen of the world"?[21] Or am I like Paul, who says, "Wretched man that I am! Who will rescue me from this body of death?" (Rom 7:24). My heart searches for the meaning of life, of the body, and of the community. As both Korean and American, but also more than either, I do not deplore my border identity. Rather, I see it as a creative marginality through which I can contribute to the redemptive healing of the scattered, battered, and ruined bodies of our people and of others in the world by reimagining a community and a world for "all."[22]

I grew up on multi-religious soil in Korea, where various religions coexist, however discordantly, and each religion leaves its distinctive marks on my soul.[23] The people of my home village lived with ancestral traditions, such as ancestor worship and the celebration of special days (for example, the Lunar New Year and Full Moon Day). Daily life, I remember, meant living in a community in which we shared even a little bread with one another in a common living space of solidarity. Even a little news spread in a second, and all people responded immediately to the needs of the community, in one way or another, giving a helping hand to the needy, weeping together in sorrow, laughing together on days of celebration. Life together seemed natural. If one hurt his leg, the community suffered, just as Paul imagines an intimate, loving relationship in the community (1 Cor 12:14-26). I also saw Buddhist monks walking through our village and heard what they taught: empty yourself; live simply; be merciful; get away from worldly desires; and do not kill living beings—even little insects. These teachings, I came to realize, corresponded to Paul's declarations that Christ emptied himself (Phil 2:7); that he learned how to live simply (Phil 4:12); that "gentleness" should be practiced toward everyone because "the Lord is near" (Phil 4:5); that we should not live according to the flesh (Rom 8:3-9); that creation itself will be set free from decay (Rom 8:21).

With this cultural background, I turn in the following pages to examine Paul's concept of the "body of Christ" with a very particular question in mind. Is it legitimate and plausible to interpret Paul's language about the "body of Christ" from a holistic religious and interreligious, intercultural outlook, rather than from an exclusivist perspective?

─────────────── **A Few Words about Method** ───────────────

Interpretation always involves the interaction of text, context, and hermeneutics.[24] There is no interpretation of the Bible that does not involve these three dimensions. Several different interpretations of a text can simultaneously be:

- legitimate (that is, can be grounded in one or another dimension of the text itself)
- plausible (that is, they can make historical or theological sense of a context)
- valid as an interpretive choice in a particular contemporary context.

Biblical criticism allows us to recognize the legitimacy and the plausibility of interpretations performed in different cultural settings with different religious perspectives. Rather than accepting as legitimate only those interpretations that reflect a Western cultural point of view or an elitist European-American academic perspective, we can account for the views and experiences of people from other classes and in other religious settings. We can choose among diverse legitimate and plausible interpretations by asking about the relative value of an interpretation and the ideological perspective it involves in a certain life-context; for example, is it liberating or oppressive? Any interpretation is a choice; and because any interpretation is contextual, a critical study must be open to an assessment of whether it is ethically healthy and communally sensitive. Critical interpreters cannot be detached; we cannot remain in splendid isolation but must assume our responsibility, with others in a particular life-context, for our interpretations and their effects.

In the following chapters, I examine various conceptions of community as "body" (Chapter 1), Pauline community as "body of Christ" (chapter 2), and Paul's understanding of community "in Christ" (chapter 3). I will show how differing scholarly approaches affect our understanding of the "body of Christ" metaphor. In chapter 4, I first will explore the body

politics of the Greco-Roman and Jewish worlds with which Paul inter-
acts and then propose a specific interpretation of the issues in Corinth
in which Paul seeks to intervene. In chapter 5, I will explore the figurative, discursive structure of 1 Corinthians, focusing on the figure of the
body, and the theological themes that emerge from three distinct body
discourses in Paul. Finally, in chapter 6, I will draw conclusions, revisiting
the issue of unity and diversity and its relation to biblical interpretation.

Fig. 1. These columns are all that remain standing of an ancient temple, built in Corinth probably in the sixth century B.C.E. The Roman destruction of the city in 146 B.C.E. damaged the temple, and subsequently the Roman colonists removed interior columns to line the colonnade entering the city. The temple was finally destroyed by an earthquake in the sixth century C.E.

CHAPTER ONE

Community as "Body"

How one conceives of community determines the way one understands the "body of Christ" in Paul. I distinguish three conceptions of community: (a) the boundary-protected community, (b) the boundaries-overcoming community, and (c) the apocalyptic community. These three conceptions of the community are all plausibly employed in scholarly interpretations of 1 Corinthians.

The conception of the *boundary-protected* community corresponds largely to theological-historical and sociological or social-scientific approaches. The notion of the boundary-protected community indicates the members' need for protection and belonging. In this understanding, the primary problem that the community addresses is a lack of identity.[1] The very existence of the community is for the sake of its members: the community provides a sense of identity, salvation, and holiness, which are *not* provided to outsiders.

The conception of the *boundaries-overcoming* community is found in the so-called New Perspective on Paul, where Paul's immediate concern is not individual salvation but a matter of relationship: how to overcome boundaries between Jews and Gentiles. According to this understanding, the key question is whether the community is inclusive or exclusive of outsiders. Paul's concern is to overcome divisive, exclusive boundaries. The very existence of the community is for the sake of others (outsiders). The difference, compared to the boundary-protected community, is that in this second view, the boundary itself does not define the community; rather, the key to understanding the community is its members' sense of vocation by which they overcome divisive boundaries.[2]

The conception of the *apocalyptic* community corresponds to an apocalyptic interpretation of Paul.[3] The notion of the apocalyptic community derives from the idea of liberation from evil powers, and the ultimate vision of the community looks to the (apocalyptic, messianic)

11

future when God will complete the messianic kingdom (1 Cor 15:20-28). Along the way, people are invited to participate in God's work.[4] The role of community here is to guide members to discern God's will so that they may continue to participate in that work.

Because my concern is with the potential for any conception of community to exclude others, my focus is especially on the first way of conceiving community, the conception of the *boundary-protected* community, which clearly excludes "others." In what follows, I will examine the emphases and ramifications of the boundary-protected community in theological-historical, sociological or social-scientific, and history-of-religions approaches. I will discuss the other two conceptions, those of the boundaries-overcoming community and the apocalyptic community, in the next chapter, where my focus will be the Pauline conception of the "body of Christ."

Community in Theological and Historical Approaches

The theological/historical approach employs the conception of the boundary-protected community that identifies the reason and purpose of the community as providing strong identity and exclusive salvation to the members of the community. The emphasis on identity and an exclusive promise of salvation to members often leads to a hegemonic universalism that excludes other ideas or other ways of thinking because "others" do not fit the ideal imagination of the "universal."[5] Likewise, "others" are excluded from the conception of the community. With this approach, there is an enthusiasm for "an ideal of a universal human essence, beyond difference and hierarchy."[6] Not surprisingly, in this view Paul is viewed as a person "motivated by a Hellenistic desire for the One."[7] The issue is how to keep a pure community of Christians who have the same ideas (unity) and the same proper identity. This concern corresponds to what we observe in the cultural, political, and philosophical agenda of nineteenth-century Germany; and it shaped modern biblical studies: namely, a search for pure or absolute truth.[8] F. C. Baur, influenced by the Hegelian dialectic of thesis-antithesis-synthesis, found a form of pure Christianity in Paul's gospel that he set over against Judaism.[9] Baur's search for "pure religion" legitimated the hegemonic voice of unity in society and the church and left no room for differences and diversity but required sameness of identity or pure unity.[10] This view of the bounded community, with a focus on pure unity and universalism, does not allow for "equality and equal rights to those who are different from this Western Christian man as the ideal of universal identity."[11]

In contrast—but sharing the same theological concern—Rudolf Bultmann read the New Testament existentially to appeal to modern readers so that they might have a sense of strong identity and meaningful existence in this unstable world.[12] That is, the purpose of the community, in Bultmann's reading, was to provide members with an authentic existence or proper identity through faith. Similarly, scholars embracing the salvation-history perspective of the New Testament held a similar conception of the boundary-protected community, focusing on a unique saving "history" with a christological center. In effect, a common sense of saving history serves as boundary-marker to which members adhere for safety's sake. For example, Johannes Munck put the history of salvation into the historical frame of the Gentile mission and reduced Paul's diverse and complex theology to a salvation-historical perspective.[13] The cost of this kind of interpretation is great, because it loses sight of the complexities of Paul's theological concerns, not to mention the complexities of the community's concerns.

——— Sociological or Social-Scientific Approaches ———

Sociological or social-scientific approaches, especially as informed by functionalism, employ the concept of the boundary-protected community in which society or the community is viewed as a metaphorical organism. In this approach, society is a living organism that has its own life.[14] Emile Durkheim, the pioneer of functionalist sociology, states that "society is nothing unless it be one, definite body, distinct from its parts."[15] Society is the only reference to which all other aspects of human existence, such as the transcendental, personal (subjective), or psychological dimension, are sacrificed. Scholars in this tradition are more concerned with how social and cultural forces determine the lives of individuals, who are considered mere reactors to these forces.[16]

A few observations regarding this school of thought are in order. First, the "sociology of knowledge" presents a "symbolic universe," a socially constructed world in which individuals must conform to social norms while being protected under a symbolic "sacred canopy."[17] In this paradigm, individuals have no voice in society and are simply swept into lives of socially constructed meanings. The problem is that the social norms tend to be tied to a hegemonic (hierarchical) voice to which individuals must conform, and that in effect brackets out their individual power to change the society. By this reductionism, one can miss the voice of the marginalized who are treated as voiceless or are invisible in the social body.[18] According to functionalist premises, we may find Paul pictured as a father (a *paterfamilias*) "responsible for exercising authority as well as maintaining order, peace and concord within his own family."[19]

—— The Approach of the History-of-Religions School ——

The conception of the boundary-protected community is also at work in some expressions of the late nineteenth- and early twentieth-century history-of-religions school that asserted that Christian faith was the only true historical religion compared with other religions and cultures. For example, Wilhelm Bousset wrote: "But—if there is to be only one religion—it is Christianity which must be the religion of the progressive nations of the earth. . . . Christianity is the only living religion that concerns us."[20] Similarly, Ernst Troeltsch wrote: "Christianity must be understood not only as the culmination point but also as the convergence point of all the developmental tendencies that can be discerned in religion. It may therefore be designated, in contrast to other religions, as the focal synthesis of all religious tendencies and the disclosure of what is in principle a new way of life."[21]

In this view, there is neither need nor room for dialogue with others. Likewise, in fusing theology with culture, Troeltsch claimed the invincibility of Christianity in Western culture: "The personalistic redemption-religion of Christianity is the highest and most significantly developed world of religious life . . . having disclosed a wealth of potentialities in its fusion with the culture of antiquity and *that of the Germanic tribes of western Europe*" (emphasis mine).[22] Similarly, Bousset stated: "We hold fast with all our power to the faith of the Gospel in a personal, heavenly Father—*a faith which conquers the world* and *rises high above this world*, yet takes us into the world and the world's work. We carry this idea of faith into our modern knowledge, into our representation of God" (emphasis mine).[23] Here one can see the double-sided character of this school. In the name of scientific, objective, and comparative (re)search, Hellenistic culture is viewed as the backdrop for a distinct form of Christianity, "Hellenistic Christianity." Bousset's claim of Christian "superiority" over the "world" —in culture or religions—is based in the conception of a boundary-protected community in which others, whether in the community or religious outsiders, are not included. Moreover, it is not any other form of Christianity but *Hellenistic* Christianity that provides true identity and salvation because it is superior to primitive "Palestinian Christianity."

Bousset argued that the use of *kyrios* (lord) in a Hellenistic cultic setting replaced the apocalyptic use of the Son of Man in Palestinian Christianity.[24] In this Hellenistic ethos, Paul was a true inheritor of the pious Hellenistic Christianity and culture in which Paul's theology and religiosity were shaped: "Thus for Paul Christ becomes the supra-terrestrial power which supports and fills with its presence his whole life. And this Christ piety of the apostle is summed up for him in the one great ever recurring formula of *en kyriō einai,*"[25] which is not derived from the earthly life of Jesus of Nazareth.[26] Likewise, Bousset advocated for a specific form of Christianity, found in piety or the spirit that tends to leave aside the ethics of Christian life based on Jesus' life and teachings. Note that Bousset's understanding of the Pauline community as a community endowing its members with benefits and characteristics not available to outsiders—that is, as a boundary-protected community—was consistent with the claim that Europe was a descendant of Hellenistic culture and Pauline Christianity, and thus superior. Bousset's claim was consistent with the attitudes of European colonialism that exhibited the same ethos of piety, while not taking into account the holy presence of God in other cultures.

In the following, by way of summary, I will talk about boundaries, identity, and power structures/relationships in the boundary-protected community, and will suggest alternative approaches to them.

Boundaries

The conception of the boundary-protected community involves a specific understanding of how boundaries work to provide identity and to shape power structures and relationships. Boundaries here refer to theologically

Fig. 2. The stout walls of the Acrocorinth citadel, rising almost 600 meters above the city, enclosed a natural spring and thus was defensible over long periods. It did not protect the city from the Roman assault of 146 B.C.E., however, which broke the strength of the Achaean League. The Romans looted and burned the city, put its men to the sword, and enslaved its women and children, leaving Corinth an insignificant village until it was resettled as a Roman colony a century later.

or socially constructed barriers based on theological identity, social functions, or social conflicts. As I have briefly outlined previously, a specific sense of identity or of salvation effectively erects boundaries between the community and outsiders. In the sociological or social-scientific approach, social functions or conflicts generate community boundaries in the same way that Gerd Theissen proposes that an ethos of "love patriarchalism" was generated in the Pauline communities; that is, an ethos of interpersonal warmth functioned to allow a few rich or upper class people to maintain the Pauline communities.[27] These theological or social boundaries remain fixed or intact due to the nature of theological or social concerns about unity and lead to a rigid, narrow, and hierarchical sense of community.[28]

The problem with this view, as I stated earlier, is that the existence of hierarchical boundaries are not questioned but are explained away by resorting either to a grand theological narrative or to the mechanisms of society in which the voice of the marginalized goes unheard. Society at the macro level decides for individuals at the micro level, as Mary Douglas's work makes clear. Accordingly, individuals have no agency to change the world or to challenge existing boundaries.[29] Boundaries at this level

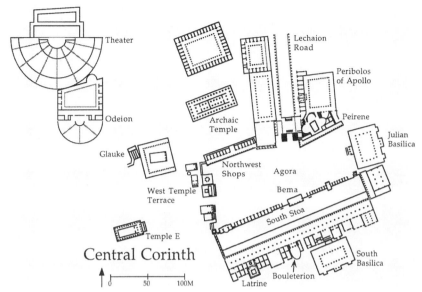

Fig 3. Having destroyed Greek Corinth, Rome later settled the site as a Roman colony. At the upper center of this plan one sees the ancient temple (see Fig. 1), now de-centered on the landscape of the city by the representation of Roman power. The main route into the city, the Lechaion Road, leads directly to the bēma, the site at which Roman justice was administered (see Acts 18:12-17). West of the bēma, the agora opens toward the most prominent sacred site in Roman Corinth, Temple E, probably dedicated to the cult of the Julian house.

are means for maintaining the community or society as a whole, based on social functions or social conflicts. Evidently, the existence or experience of the marginalized never receives full attention in social-science or sociological approaches, because in these approaches the marginalized are invisible and hidden behind the powerful people in society or in the community.

I doubt that Paul would have supported the idea of love patriarchalism in the Corinthian community. Though I agree with the so-called New Consensus that Paul's community was composed of a cross-section of the urban population ranging from slaves to the upper class, I do not agree that Paul held such a conservative social view as that projected by functionalism, which would have allowed hierarchical boundaries in the community (for example, between the rich and the poor).[30] Actually, our view of Paul changes if we conceive of the community differently, that is, as a radical community of *all,* based on Paul's deconstruction and reconstruction of

Fig. 4. Anyone entering the Roman temple honoring the house of Julius Caesar and Augustus (Temple E) might have looked up to see this pediment bust overhead. The city of Corinth is personified as the Roman goddess Fortuna (Greek Tychē*); her crown is formed by the walls of the city (now restored following the city's destruction at Roman hands).*

the "body of Christ" in a specific historical context. In this view, one can read Paul as a strong advocate for egalitarianism based on a radical theology of Christ crucified. This picture of an egalitarian community is plausible when one reads the voice of the marginalized in the community and society. In this view, the central question is not only *who* comprises the Pauline communities, but also how we understand the dynamics of the community in view of Paul's radical theology of Christ crucified (an issue to which I will return in chapter 4).

The alternate approach that I take questions the ideological construction of boundaries by asking: "Who gets to set boundaries? Who is in control?" Along with a suspicion of boundaries, some feminists defy the fixing of boundaries of any sort, asserting "the deeply haunting presence of *ambivalence* and *ambiguity* which runs through all attempts of interpretation and existential transformations."[31] Feminist or liberation movements challenge any such strong boundary constructed by men or elites and challenge a traditional notion of the community that is based on hierarchy and the legitimation of unequal power relationships.[32] From their perspective, there should be no definite, absolute, or permanent boundaries by which some people are excluded.[33] Rather, boundaries should blur and change to include everyone in the conception of the community and in its practices.[34]

Identity

I understand identity to involve both an individual and collective sense of *who we are* in the community. To those who focus on the theological/historical approach, personal identity remains fixed and singular, depending on where one belongs. Personal identity is established or labeled by belonging to a specific group; members are to follow certain norms to stay in the community. However, as Tan Yah-Hwee observes, there is no clearcut dividing line between one identity and another. In her multicultural context of Singapore, a dichotomous "either/or" view of identity between Christian and Chinese is misleading.[35] For instance, regarding the discussion in 1 Corinthians of eating food offered to idols, Tan argues that identity is decided not by who is right or wrong (either/or); rather, identity emerges through the dialogue of community relationships where the naming of identity by fighting for who is right or wrong leads nowhere.[36] The key point is that a rigid sectarian mentality of belonging is outweighed by a communal view of relation with others in a complex community with many competing assertions and ideologies.[37]

In the sociological, social-scientific approach as well, identity remains singular or fixed. The only difference, as compared with the theological approach, is the way that identity is defined. In the case of the theological/historical approach, identity is defined in terms of theological or historical categories, whereas in the sociological approach, sociological categories define identity. We can imagine an alternate approach, however, in which identity is thought of in terms of a multiple identity that rejects any singular construction. Through the demise of fixed, singular, monolithic identity politics, this alternate approach views identity as a floating, "intervening space."[38] One's identity is constantly re-created as a new hybridity in dialogue with others in the community and society.[39]

Structure or Power Relationships

In the theological/historical approach, as we saw with Bousset and Baur, there is a clear sense of hierarchical relationship within the community, with the conviction that a unique, historical revelation is established and handed down through the "rightful" (or theocratic) leadership of the church. There is also a sense of hierarchy embedded in the understanding of the church as an agent of God, a bearer of truth, with an ultimate power over the world.[40] Consequently, there is a perception of hierarchy in church and in society with a notion that the world is God's, and that therefore the church takes center stage in the world.[41] The sense of theocracy in which Jesus' brothers represented God's power was strong in the Jerusalem church, for example. David Odell-Scott notes the problem of theocracy in the contemporary interpretation of Paul's letters as well, pointing to the inappropriate English translation *church*, derived from the Greek *kyriakē*, meaning "belonging to the Lord"—a theocratic meaning inconsistent with Paul's understanding of *ekklēsia*.[42] In Paul's day Jerusalem-centered brothers (leaders) associated with Jesus' brothers could exercise such power among many Gentile churches. Ironically, this theological/historical approach does not have a strong voice of resistance or protest against social injustice or corruption, in part because social issues are considered peripheral or secondary to salvation, and principally because salvation is understood to be found only or primarily within the church. This sort of silence and/or a lack of resistance actually perpetuates the internal hierarchical structure of the community by condoning the very same hierarchical, abusive power in society that then aggravates the marginalization of women, the poor, and the weak.

In contrast, the sociological, social-scientific approach does not lead to the same aspects of theocracy in the sense that God rules through representatives. But it, too, presupposes a hierarchical structure in the community based on social functions or conflicts.[43] This structure is "a unified system of beliefs and practices . . . which unite into one single moral community called a church, all those who adhere to them."[44] The sociological analysis of social functions in a given society does not fully cover or account for the diversity or complexity in society and the community.

In an alternate approach, the central questions are not who is "in" and who is "out," but who defines the community? Who writes history?[45] Do equality, freedom, or justice exist in the community and society?[46] To apply these questions to the Pauline assemblies, feminist scholars examine both text and readers, exposing the androcentric and/or patriarchal construction of the Christian communities by contemporary scholars.[47] The broad-based conception of the community includes *all*[48]—based not on an "either/or" or "inside/outside" notion of the community but on an inclusive notion of encompassing "all differences" in the community.[49]

Thus, all kinds of politics, including identity politics,[50] should be tested through the prism of diversity and differentiation.[51] On the other hand, the postmodern, postcolonial, and feminist understandings of community should not be monolithic but diverse, complex, and with a notion of hybridity.[52] In this regard, one should allow for a creative "intervening space," in which people struggle to locate themselves in encountering others, and begin to identify common goals without sacrificing the creative tensions of living in ambiguity and uncertainty in our lives.[53]

The Conception of Community Called for in Our Present Context

In this chapter, we have examined the conception of community as boundary-protected, that is, in terms of a rigid, narrow vision of the community constituted through the exclusion of "others." In the context of a deepening fragmentation of the world today, we need to embrace a different conception of community—a community of all in diversity and solidarity. I believe such a conception is available in Paul's new imagination of the body of Christ as a collective participation in *Christ crucified*.[54] In that community, the image of Christ crucified deconstructs the conception of the community based on powers of wealth, status, and identity and reconstructs the community based on sacrificial love and solidarity with those who are *broken* in society. This power of the cross—a different kind of power altogether—challenges the whole notion of the community based on "either/or" language of belonging and exclusion and makes possible a new formation of the community of *all* in diversity.

CHAPTER TWO

Community as the "Body of Christ"

The three conceptions of community discussed in chapter 1 correspond to three approaches to Paul's language of the "body of Christ." The conception of the *boundary-protected* community has to do with an understanding of the body of Christ as an ecclesiological organism. The conception of the *boundaries-overcoming* community corresponds with the corporate-solidarity approach of the New Perspective. And the conception of the *apocalyptic* community corresponds with a christological interpretation of the phrase. Among these approaches, the ecclesiological-organic approach deserves particular attention because a majority of Paul's interpreters have read his metaphor of the "body of Christ" narrowly in terms of a call for an organic unity in the community (*homonoia*).[1] But by reducing the "body of Christ" to a mere ecclesiological organism, this approach makes an implicitly exclusive claim about the "body of Christ" as boundary marker. In contrast, the other two approaches to Paul's phrase oppose reducing its meaning to that of a mere ecclesiological organism and instead view the "body of Christ" as referring to Christ's work.[2]

The Body of Christ as Organic Unity

A number of scholars understand Paul's reference to the community as the "body of Christ" as a call for unity in terms of an organic metaphor. Richard A. Horsley views the Corinthian "body" as a metaphor for a social organism that plays the role of anti-imperial resistance.[3] For Horsley, the primary issues of the community relate to survival in the face of threats, persecution, and other difficulties of life under the Roman Empire.[4] Thus, he reads the "body of Christ" as a site of anti-imperial resistance and accordingly views *ekklēsia* as a counterassembly to the assembly of society. This resistant reading has the merit of representing the Corinthian church as a struggling community seeking justice. However, there is no distinction between the "body of Christ" and the *ekklēsia;* as a result, the possibility that the "body of Christ" might incorporate diversity is sacrificed.

Employing an explicitly sociological method, Gerd Theissen reads the Corinthian "body" as a site of "love patriarchalism,"[5] Theissen's term for an ethos that mirrors the conservative, hierarchically bound ethos of Roman society.[6] For him, the metaphor "body of Christ" provides social cohesion for the different classes in the community. As a result, hierarchy in the Corinthian community is not questioned.

Relying on sociological and anthropological categories, Jerome Neyrey sees the Corinthian "body" as a "bounded system" of a symbolic world.[7] Influenced by Mary Douglas's book *Purity and Danger* on cultural anthropology,[8] Neyrey reads the "body of Christ" as "a bounded system" in which disorder or disunity is not allowed for the community.[9] Paul asks the community to control the social body. In this reading, the human body is a sociological, psychological reality corresponding to the social body and intrinsically connected with outside social forces. But the role of human agency or subjectivity is reduced to a receptive passivity. Ultimately, this anthropological reading focuses on concern for the social boundary rather than on problems of hierarchy, injustice, and inequality internal to the community.

Based on her exploration of the tradition of upper-class Greco-Roman rhetoric,[10] Margaret Mitchell reads Paul's discourse of the "body of Christ" as an appeal for unity and concord (*homonoia*) in the community, at the price of diversity.[11] Mitchell reads 1 Corinthians as fitting a wider pattern of deliberative rhetorical discourse that sought to establish *homonoia* (concord).[12] Thus, she reads "body of Christ" as a metaphor for an ecclesiological organism in the way society is a social body in Stoic *homonoia* speeches. "Body of Christ" also serves as a boundary marker that distinguishes those who are in Christ and those who are not. The purpose of the boundary is to fend off dangers of immoral life or to remove factions or divisions in the community. In this approach, one can hear only the echo of elite voices (the strong) concerned about unity, but not other echoes of women, slaves, the weak, and of other marginalized people.[13] Mitchell considers factionalism as the cause of disunity but does not ask why factionalism occurred (a question that would have raised a marginalized perspective). As a result, her reading of the "body of Christ" does not take into account the diversity and complexity of a community struggling with the issues of power, injustice, and control. A more pointed hermeneutical question is: Is unity the solution to the problems in this community and society?

In a similar reading, Robert Gundry emphasizes the theological unity expressed in the "body of Christ."[14] The historic revelation of the Christ event unifies all members of the church in Christ. Criticizing Rudolf Bultmann's individualistic interpretation of the phrase, Gundry relates the "body of Christ" to the earthly church and to the community of members.[15] This reading is similar to C. K. Barrett's understanding of 1 Corinthians as a work of systematic theology addressing a single situation of community fragmentation that must be resolved through unity.[16] Without explicitly evoking the *homonoia* speech of the Greco-Roman body politic, Barrett understands that the metaphor of the "body of Christ" refers to the Corinthian church as an ecclesiological organism. He reads 1 Cor 12:12-27 in terms of a body analogy common in ancient society and at the same time, considers Paul's authority and power as the basis for the unity of the community.

The Body of Christ as Corporate Solidarity

What I will call the corporate-solidarity approach emphasizes a corporate body—a larger conception of the community, potentially including all of humanity, as evident in Paul's Christ-Adam typology. I include in this approach the works of E. Schweizer, Wheeler Robinson, and W. D. Davies. This approach owes much to Wheeler Robinson's discussion of the corporate body which has primacy over individuals.[17] Robinson described the characteristics of a corporate personality:[18]

(1) the unity of its extension both into the past and into the future; (2) the characteristic "realism" of the conception, which distinguishes it from "personification," and makes the group a real entity actualized in its members; (3) the fluidity of reference, facilitating rapid and unmarked transitions from the one to the many, and from

the many to the one; (4) the maintenance of the corporate idea even after the development of a new individualistic emphasis within it.

The idea of a "corporate" body informs Paul's discussion of the Second Adam (Jesus) that re-forms the community of God's people. Because of its overall emphasis on continuity and solidarity with the entirety of human beings as a body, this approach tends to have a broader conception of the community than the other approach emphasizing organic unity. Similarly, W. D. Davies sees the "body of Adam" as including all those who are in Adam, just as all must be unified in Christ: Greek and Jew, male and female. Adam symbolically represents a real oneness of humankind (the "body" of Adam including all humankind), so the "body of Christ," the new Adam, represents the oneness of the new humanity incorporated in Christ.[19] Using symbolism and an intertextual dimension, he finds a strong connection between the corporate nature of the body of Adam and of Christ. This approach has a potentially broader scope than the closed boundary of the first understanding.

In the same vein, Eduard Schweizer views Adam as a patriarchal figure representing all humans and thus sees Christ's body including all in Christ through "substantival subjectivity in the form of activity in the concrete world."[20] For him, the problem is a lack of participation in Christ, especially a lack of participation with the cross of Christ, which is a universal mission mandated by Christ.[21] Interpreting the "body of Christ" "as a missionary body, that is, as an extension of the incarnation through evangelistic activity," he views the mission of the universal church body as service; and he reads the metaphor of the body as part of *parenesis* directed to achieving this mission by emphasizing the physical realism of the "body of Christ" on the cross.[22] Schweizer states that the congregation is dependent on the historical Christ event; so the "body of Christ" cannot be reduced to physical identification with the church.[23] Alternatively, he reads the "body of Christ" as the body on the cross, emphasizing the historical salvific event of Christ on which Christians depend.

Christological Approaches

The christological approach to the "body of Christ" similarly emphasizes the role of Christ, which is central to God's apocalyptic drama. The "body of Christ" as Christ's own body does not refer to the church or to the community, but to the prior union of each believer with Christ through the lordship of Christ (Ernst Käsemann),[24] or through participation in the messianic kingdom of God, as Albert Schweitzer states, describing the bodily union between the believer and Christ:[25]

> The enigmatic concept, which dominates [Paul's] mysticism, of the "body of Christ" to which all believers belong, and in which they are already dead and risen again, is thus derived from the pre-existent Church (the "Community of God"). . . . The relationship of faith in Christ to union with Christ is for [Paul] thus: that belief in Christ being present, union with Christ automatically takes place under certain circumstances, that is to say, when the believer causes himself [*sic*] to be baptized. . . . The peculiarity of the Pauline mysticism is precisely that being-in-Christ is not a subjective experience brought about by a special effort of faith on the part of believer, but something which happens, in him as in others, at baptism.

For Schweitzer, "the Elect [individual believers] no longer carry on an independent existence, but are now only the Body of Christ," in which the Elect "form a joint personality, in which the peculiarities of the individuals, such as are constituted by race and sex and social position, have no longer any validity."[26] However, Schweitzer makes it clear that the *ethics* of "being-in-Christ" has nothing to do with Pauline mysticism; so he warns:[27]

> The great danger for all mysticism is that of becoming supra-ethical, that is to say, of making the spirituality associated with the being-in-eternity an end itself. . . . Even in Christian Mysticism, whether medieval or modern, it is often the semblance of ethics rather than ethics itself which is preserved. There is always the danger that the mystic will experience the eternal as absolute impassivity, and will consequently cease to regard the ethical existence as the highest manifestation of spirituality.

Schweitzer "expounds his [Paul's] ethic as the putting into operation of the dying and rising again with Christ" as in Gal 5:13–6:10 and Romans 5:1–8:17.[28] In the former passage, Paul exhorts the Galatians to return to their life in Spirit by deserting the works of the flesh.[29] In the latter, Paul's

ethic calls for enduring suffering and dying with Christ in order to be
"purified and liberated from the world."[30] As such, Paul's ethics emphasizes
the action, suffering, and liberation (from the world) as Paul formulates
the "essential character of the ethical" in ways that exemplify "sanctification, giving up the service of sin, living for God, bringing forth fruit for
God, serving the Spirit."[31] Notably, Schweitzer shifts from a view of the
"body of Christ" metaphor as referring merely to individual participation
in a social organism to a view of participation in the "body of Christ" centered on soteriology and ethics, and focuses on a kind of apocalyptic ethics
of the present in which believers now live and die with Christ. He does
so by distinguishing Pauline mysticism from the subjective, supra-divine
experience of Hellenistic mysticism.[32]

Ernst Käsemann is also suspicious of the identification of the "body
of Christ" as church or human institution;[33] the church is not simply the
"body of Christ," as he clearly states:[34]

> The unavoidable starting point seems to me the necessity of breaking
> away from the view once current (at least among Protestants), that
> in describing the church as the body of Christ, Paul, who inclined to
> bold statements, was using a beautiful metaphor.[35] . . . The influence
> of the Stoic notion of organism, which (as in Menenius Agrippa's
> famous fable) permits a community to be described as a body, will
> hardly be denied by anyone, especially since 1 Cor 12:14ff is clearly
> a reflection of it. But this is hardly enough, in view of the statement
> in 1 Cor 12:12, with its sacramental substantiation in the following
> verse. For Paul does not simply establish the fact that the church is a
> body; the argument is a Christological one, as in Rom 12:4: it is with
> Christ himself (to take the most cautious interpretation) as it is with
> the body; 'in Christ' the church is a body.

As seen previously, Käsemann shifts the importance of the metaphor
to the obedience of the church to the rule of Christ and the Spirit enacted
through sacrament.[36] In other words, the lordship of Christ extends to the
cosmic level, and it is a new age, "a new world or, better, a new creation in
universal dimension."[37] Käsemann makes the further distinction between
Christ and the church, writing that "Christ is there before the church and
he is not absorbed into that church."[38] Accordingly, Käsemann reads the
metaphor "body of Christ" as *parenesis*. That is to say, the "body of Christ"

is not the church itself but Christ's body with which believers are united so that they might live a somatic life, in all aspects of worldly relations. He elaborates on this notion of the church as a conduit:[39]

> To put it somewhat too epigrammatically, the apostle is not interested in the church *per se* and as a religious group. He is only interested in it in so far as it is the means whereby Christ reveals himself on earth and becomes incarnate in the world through his Spirit. The human body is the necessity and reality of existential communication; in the same way, the church appears as the possibility and reality of communication between the risen Christ and our world, and hence is called his body. It is the sphere in which and through which Christ proves himself *Kyrios* on earth after his exaltation. It is the body of Christ as his present sphere of sovereignty, in which he deals with the world through Word, sacrament and the sending forth of Christians, and in which he finds obedience even before his parousia.

Käsemann states that "the motif of the body of Christ in Paul only crops up in parenetic contexts,"[40] whereas in the Deutero-Pauline letters, "the doxological way of speaking about the 'body of Christ' is dominant."[41] Furthermore, the rule of Christ through the Spirit extends to the whole cosmos because of his theological view of the "body of Christ." Overall, Käsemann's notion of *sōma* remains the same as Bultmann's, but his view of the "body of Christ" has a transcendental origin, and thus it is "a transcendent aeon or sphere"[42] (although Käsemann insists that Paul counters the Gnostic use of *sōma*).[43] Nonetheless, it is important to recognize his contributions in terms of his careful distinction between the church and the body of Christ and his ethical sensitivity to reading the body of Christ in a parenetic context.

Summary and Critique

As we consider these three approaches to the metaphor "body of Christ," my concern is with interpretations that leave no room for contemplating the marginalized and give no account of the value of diversity. In my view, the christological approach and the corporate-solidarity approach do hold potential for addressing our issues, but fail to actualize that potential.

On the other hand, we must reject the ecclesiological organism approach because it leaves no room for taking into account marginalized voices or diversity. The christological approach has a critical, contextual consciousness about the apocalyptic character of the present time, but its vision of the community and Christian life are limited to the category of a traditional Christian theology; thus "others" are excluded in the name of forensic salvation *by faith*. With the notion of "universalism" through faith in Christ, this approach fails to embrace diversity or give an account of the full value of living in relation with those who are genuinely other. In contrast, the corporate-solidarity approach seems to embrace a larger conception of the community—potentially including all humanity—with the theme of solidarity or reconciliation. However, there is not much room for conceptualizing intercultural or interreligious encounters in this interpretation because solidarity is based on a typology of Christ alone. The ecclesiological-organic approach most rigidly conceives of the community as a "unity" that denies differences or diversity.[44]

Alternately, I propose that we can read 1 Corinthians through the angle of diversity and difference by refusing to read this letter as a single voice of deliberative rhetoric. Rather, 1 Corinthians can be legitimately understood as a multi-voiced *textus,* woven through Paul's replies to the concerns of the Corinthians (both in written letters and verbal reports to Paul).[45] As such, we can reconstruct bits and pieces of Paul's handling of the Corinthian conflicts differently from the socio-rhetorical reading that emphasizes unity as the chief value. We must ask why scholars who embrace the ecclesiological organism view of "body of Christ" hear in the dialogue between Paul and the Corinthian community only the elite voice of the *homonoia* (concord) speech that is used to maintain the status quo in society? The answer, I submit, is that in much of the tradition of received interpretation, the "body of Christ" has long been held captive, while serving ecclesial interests and legitimizing the powerful in society and the church. The fossilized "body of Christ" as a metaphor for a unified organism precludes other possibilities of meaning that would open the opportunity for cross-cultural dialogue with "others."

To realize an alternative interpretation, we must turn away from reading the letter as elite discourse (in the form of hierarchical unity) and discern the minority voices woven into the text, as we do more readily when we read from the perspective of the marginalized, rather than with the elite and the powerful who strive to maintain the status quo. References to the experiences of the marginalized in the text are clear and powerful. The weak in the Corinthian community (1:27; 4:10) should be empowered through the gospel of Christ because they are also people of God. For the mission of God's love for the weak and the marginalized, Paul was called as "a slave to all" (9:19). For this call and mission, Paul considers himself "the rubbish of the world" (4:13) because he also goes through Christ-like life and death. Paul utterly identifies with Christ crucified (1:23; 2:2), which is God's power and wisdom that deconstructs the Corinthian power and wisdom based on a certain knowledge or special gifts. Christ's body imagined through Christ crucified gives hope to the weak and marginalized in the community, even in the midst of their liminal, marginal experience— just as Christ necessarily did. Christ crucified is a symbol and the power of God reaching out to the downtrodden, the dregs of the world. In short, accounting for the crucified body as a dimension of the "body of Christ" provides us with a vision of the "body of Christ" in radical association with the broken bodies in the world.

Conceiving the "Body of Christ" in a Cruciform Reality

A new conception of community in the context of marginalization and social fragmentation requires that we imagine anew the Pauline "body of Christ" as a social site for realizing the ethical, holistic, and life-giving potentialities of Christ's life and death. In particular, the image of Christ crucified may be seen as deconstructing powers and ideologies of wealth, status, or belonging and reconstructing the community through sacrificial love.[46] The actual, ideal reconstruction of the Corinthian loving community appears in 1 Cor 13–14, where Paul emphasizes that *ekklēsia* is a matter of participation in *sōma christou* (Christ's life and death) for *all* members of the community. This notion of the "body of Christ" envisions a community that negates hegemony and affirms diversity. In a nutshell, the "body of Christ" in the present context of marginality and fragmentation of the world includes *all*, which is possible through the living of Christ because one can identify with Christ's life and death in a most concrete context.

CHAPTER THREE

Community "in Christ"

The famous phrase "in Christ" (*en christō*) in Paul's letters is often understood as a boundary marker that reinforces ecclesiological unity, corresponding to the way the metaphorical language of "body of Christ" is read by many as a metaphor for the organic unity of the church. Actually, the interpretation of the phrase is much more complex than normally imagined. For instance, the dative construction of *en christō* can be understood in many different ways.[1] The dative may indicate spatial relationships; instrumental relationships, indicating the means by which something occurs; temporal relationships describing the time "during, in, or within" which something occurs; or modal relationships, describing circumstances or manner.

Adolph Deissmann reads the phrase as a reference to the mystical union or relationship of the individual with Christ, absent any sense of an ethical interpretation.[2] At the other end of that spectrum, replacing the subjective, mystical language with an emphasis on God's work *in Christ*,[3] Fritz Neugebauer reads the phrase through an ecclesiological lens: the eschatological event that takes place "in Christ" makes possible the true community of believers.[4] In this reading, "in Christ" serves as a boundary marker to exclude others in the conception of the community. Similarly, C. H. Dodd emphasizes this local reading of the phrase as a boundary marker: "to be baptized" is the same as "to be in Christ," and "to be in Christ" is "to be in the church."[5] Albert Schweitzer strikes a balance between these two extremes—personal, mystical union and ecclesiological unity.[6] For him, "in Christ" points to the quality of an eschatological life here and now and the messianic community in Christ. For Schweitzer, to be "in Christ" is to live the eschatological time here and now "in Christ."[7] Similarly, Ernst Käsemann emphasizes an ethical Christian life through the lordship of Christ.[8]

Among many possibilities for interpreting "in Christ" or the related expression "in the Lord," reading the phrase as a boundary marker has been dominant for a long time, coupled with an ecclesiological reading of the "body of Christ." A typical case can be found in 1 Cor 7:39, where Paul declares that a widow may remarry "only in the Lord" (*monon en kyriō*). Many scholars interpret *monon en kyriō* as limiting the widow's remarriage to a fellow Christian.[9] Among these interpreters are Tertullian, Cyprian, Jerome, and Calvin, to name a few.[10] Likewise, the New International Version translates it: "A woman is bound to her husband as long as he lives. But if her husband dies, she is free to marry anyone she wishes, but he must *belong to* the Lord." We can certainly read it that way, given the cultural, social setting in the first century C.E., when marriage outside the same social group was unthinkable.[11] But Paul declares that just the reverse is acceptable. That is, he does not oppose marriage outside the same social group, as we see in 1 Cor 7:12-14. On the contrary, Paul has a positive view about mixed marriage because according to him, a believing spouse will effect the sanctification of an unbelieving spouse: "For the unbelieving husband is made holy through his wife, and the unbelieving wife is made holy through her husband. Otherwise, your children would be unclean, but as it is, they are holy" (7:14).[12] Read this way, a different set of ethical possibilities emerge. That is, "only in the Lord" can be an open-ended invitation and exhortation to live like Christ, because the dative case "in the Lord" can be understood as "instrumental,"—by the power, or life of, the Lord.

Though his language primarily focuses on "existentialism," Rudolf Bultmann also read 1 Corinthians from the perspective that *en Christō* marked the boundary of an ecclesiological organism: "to belong to the Christian church is to be 'in Christ' or 'in the Lord' . . . and Christian congregations may also be called congregations *in Christ*."[13] Here we see his contextual concerns about security and identity, living in the midst of chaos and instability. But these kinds of concern for "belonging" result in too narrow a conception of the community. Reading "in Christ" as a boundary marker emphasizes the notion of unity at the price of diversity or of an open-ended notion of community. Thus the phrase "you in (of) Christ" (1 Cor 3:23; similarly in 15:22) is understood as "belonging to Christ" (that is, to the church or the community) and having the same mind (being in unity). Paul's statement in Gal 3:28 that in Christ "there is no longer Jew or Greek, there is no longer slave or free, there is no longer male and female; for all of you are one in Christ Jesus" can also be understood as eradicating differences or diversity. That is, "in Christ" points to a "universal body," one which sacrifices a deeper, ethical meaning of Pauline theology and ethics.[14] As Ricardo Garcia observes, it may also become "a weapon for cultural imperialism"[15] as members of the community *in Christ* are encouraged to maintain the same mind, as in a "melting pot theory of assimilation"[16] without the acceptance of cultural or convictional differences.[17]

Inevitably, when "in Christ" is read as a boundary marker, it contributes to a narrow or an exclusive vision of the community that separates Christians from non-Christians.[18] In this way, "in the Lord" of 1 Cor 7:39 is invariably read as prohibiting widows from remarrying non-Christians.[19] Only those who are "in Christ"—within the "body of Christ" (as the church)—are guaranteed proper identity or salvation.[20] In this view it is difficult to conceptualize engagement with "others."

I propose an alternate reading of "in Christ" in 1 Corinthians, based on a different conception of the Corinthian context that foregrounds not a position of power but the perspective of marginality.

An Alternative Reading of "in Christ" in 1 Corinthians

I conceive of the community "in Christ"[21] as an "intervening space"[22] or as "a gathering of differences"[23] from the perspective of postmodern imagination.[24] Likewise, we may conceive "in Christ" as referring to a social space for struggling or a time for meaningful existence here and now in the midst of turmoil because Christ's life and death ("in Christ" as modal relation) deconstructs the power ideologies of some Corinthians and reconstructs the community (*ekklēsia*) for all.[25] This understanding of the community as a creative, struggling space for justice allows us to recognize the conflicting voices in the Corinthian context—conflicts between those whom Paul sarcastically calls "wise in Christ" (4:10) and those who are "sanctified in Christ Jesus" (1:2). The "wise in Christ" seek to maintain their power through wisdom or knowledge while considering those "who are sanctified in Christ Jesus" to be foolish enough not to claim their own place as such. The "strong" (variously characterized as the rich, the knowledgeable, the wise, and the enthusiasts) claim that they are "wise in Christ" (4:10-16) and reject the message of Christ crucified because it seems to them the most foolish way of life (1:18–2:16). Instead, they promote their own ideology of unity as unilateralism or individualism, not recognizing that Christ died as an effect of such uncaring and divisive ideologies.[26] These "strong" people reject Paul's ministry of reconciliation grounded in the death of Christ, egalitarianism, and diversity.[27] In fact, the aim of the strong is to unify the whole community under their hegemonic power *in Christ*, as we see the divisions of Corinthians based on each group's claim that they are true representatives of God's church in Christ.[28] The central cause of divisions has to do with leading ideologies associated with names to which some people belong: "Paul, Apollos, Cephas, and Christ" (1 Cor 1:12).

In response, Paul sarcastically accepts his own role as foolishness on behalf of Christ.[29] Paul refutes the use of "in Christ" language as a boundary marker.[30] Instead, Paul identifies himself with the most foolish people: "[W]hen slandered, we speak kindly. We have become like the rubbish of the world, the dregs of all things, to this very day" (4:13).[31] Paul's sarcasm represents a rhetoric of protest against the dominant oppressive systems of the world; systems that suffocate the powerless and make them hungry. Paul's protesting voice also aims more immediately at the internal community divided by the various ideologies of power brokers. With this voice of resistance and protest, aimed both internally and externally, slaves, the oppressed, and the poor should claim their own place in the community and society. Whereas the dominant ideology in society generates a centripetal force of hierarchical unity, Paul's theology of "in Christ" is centrifugal, acting as a force for God's love for all people—especially for the downtrodden. Through the image of Christ crucified, Paul deconstructs the ideology of "unity" on the part of "the strong" and reconstructs a community based on the cross.[32]

"In Christ" as a Modal Relation: *Dying with Christ*

In contrast to the unity-based, belonging-centered reading of "in Christ," Paul's language of "Christ's dying" shows that the same phrase can be read modally. That is, the phrase can refer to a way of life manifested in and associated with Christ's life and sacrifice (Christ's dying).[33] Paul says he dies every day with Christ (15:31), not accepting or condoning oppression or torture, but confronting or overcoming the self-seeking powers that oppress, marginalize, and torture others. Paul speaks of suffering from all sorts of adversity: from torture, degradation, and persecution in society. For Paul to die with Christ is more than an individual experience of mystical spirituality; it has to do with sharing the experience of the one who suffers the death of a slave, who experiences the extreme limits of human suffering and rejection. In other words, when Paul talks about Christ crucified (1:23; 2:2), he probably thinks of the slave's death, too, and of the slave's life, which is a daily shame and a liminal experience between life and death.[34]

Therefore, *in Christ* one can experience the margins of humanity. Based on this understanding of Paul's radical identification with Christ crucified, one can see Paul's emphatic theology of dying with Christ and sharing it with others in their most unfortunate situations. As such, Christ crucified or "dying with Christ" should not be romanticized or spiritualized at an individual, psychological, existential, or mystical level. For Paul, these phrases refer to participating with the lowly through Christ. In that sense, for Paul the cross is not a once-and-for-all event that guarantees "salvation" through a substitutionary death of Jesus.[35] For Paul, dying with Christ is a realistic, radical sharing of the experiences of those who suffer like Christ. Accordingly, Paul reminds the community of his "ways in Christ Jesus" (4:17). Paul can recommend that widows remarry "in the Lord," which is not a language of belonging but an expression that reflects a Christ-like attitude and commitment to live a way of life marked by dying (7:39). Paul declares that all shall be made alive through/in Christ. That is, all people can live as God's people when their lives are challenged and empowered by Christ's sacrificial love. On the other hand, all die *in Adam,* who represents the old life—unlike Christ's life—because they live for themselves only (15:22).[36]

As we have seen thus far, a traditional theological approach to Paul's "in Christ" language fossilizes Christian identity, fixes it as exclusive, and removes any possibility of a genuine, open-ended engagement with others or of seeing community in multiple contexts and through the lens of diversity. Because of concerns and issues that I raised in the Introduction, I propose to read "in Christ" and the language of the "body of Christ" as referring to a new space and time.[37] The primary space and time of our thinking and acting is not simply fixed, abstract, or linear, but changing, concrete, and circular.[38] This new space and time can be termed the "third space" of a community that is struggling toward liberation and justice for all.[39] This space and time is not given from "above" but is realized when humans live in that struggling space and time.[40]

In summary, among many choices readers make, I choose to read from a perspective of diversity and thus to read the phrase "in Christ" modally, as describing a way of life that is participation in Christ's life. This vision of community deconstructs the ideologies of powers through the image of Christ crucified (1 Cor 1:27-31) and reconstructs the life of diversity as living like Christ. This sense of "living Christ" allows for the totality of God's involvement in our life, with a humble recognition that truths lie also with others, and that truths are provisional and confessional (see 1 Cor 13:9-13).[41] First Corinthians 13 elevates the importance of love in the community; the language of love used here is not noun but verb, which emphasizes the Corinthians' action to build this community of love in their concrete life context.

CHAPTER FOUR

The Body Politic and the Body of Christ

How can we account for the relation between Paul and his social, political world? How do we know what we know about Paul's philosophical context or background? Many scholars readily align Paul's language of the body with the learned school of Stoicism, for which one pillar of thought was unity and harmony—a hierarchical form of unity purchased at the cost of many lowly people, including slaves. These scholars consider the body politic of Stoicism to be the fundamental source of Paul's ideas and actions and therefore read 1 Corinthians as a plea for the unity of the ecclesiological organism, as I have shown in previous chapters.[1]

But although that political reality certainly existed, so did others. Paul's theology of Christ crucified evokes the bodies of crucified slaves and the experience of those considered nothing in the Greco-Roman world, as we read his emphasis on God's radical love for the marginalized in 1 Cor 1:26-31:

> Consider your own call, brothers and sisters: not many of you were wise by human standards, not many were powerful, not many were of noble birth. But God chose what is foolish in the world to shame the wise; God chose what is weak in the world to shame the strong; God chose what is low and despised in the world, things that are not, to reduce to nothing things that are, so that no one might boast in the presence of God. He is the source of your life in Christ Jesus, who became for us wisdom from God, and righteousness and sanctification and redemption, in order that, as it is written, "Let the one who boasts, boast in the Lord.

Indeed, Paul compares himself with the liminal experiences of the marginalized: "We have become like the rubbish of the world, the dregs of all things, to this very day" (4:9-13). These observations suggest that Pauline scholarship today should look for indications of the marginalized in the letter's context. Here, therefore, I reexamine the body politic of the Greco-Roman and the Jewish world with sensitivity to the voice of the socially marginalized. One of the pivotal hermeneutical questions is: Whose voice does Paul side with among the various conflicting voices in the world?

I investigate various body-related issues in First Corinthians, ranging from the issue of division to resurrection. I show how we can read First Corinthians with a different understanding of its context.

The Body Politic in the Greco-Roman and Ancient Jewish Worlds

The Politics of the Hegemonic Body

The politics of the hegemonic body represented the voices of the aristocrats and the Roman Empire, with roots in Plato and Aristotle.[2] Plato (472–347 B.C.E.) in *Phaedo* establishes a hierarchical dualism[3] in which the soul takes priority over the body, which serves as the prison for the soul.[4] Plato's *Timaeus* expounds his theory of the hierarchical cosmic body in which differing forms (*ideas*) of living bodies exist in the universe.[5] Plato further divides the soul into three parts: the reasonable (*logistikon*), the courageous (*thumoeides*), and the appetitive (*epithumetikon*).[6] The first part is eternal and immortal; the other two parts are mingled with the material body. The varying degrees of combinations of the soul and material body determine the ranks of men and things in the world. Plato describes his highly stratified ideal state as one in which the philosophers become the rulers because they are supposed to have the higher soul.[7] According to him, the human body is also hierarchically structured; the head is the most divine part of the body and rules the rest of the body.[8] The head, the superior part, represents the male, whereas the female constitutes the weaker part of humanity.[9] Barbarians and slaves are less human.[10]

Aristotle's view is similar to Plato's in the sense that both promote the hierarchical view of the cosmos and humans alike. Aristotle's worldview centers on *nous* (mind) as the divine element. Male is superior to female, a

Fig. 5. Glimpses of the elite of Roman Corinth. *This inscription honors "Junia Polla, daughter of Publius, wife of Gaius Julius Lectus. After her death colonists [of Corinth gave this] by decree of the decuriones." Junia was a common enough name in the first century C.E. (see Rom 16:7); the quality of this monument, in marble, indicates that Junia was a woman of some importance.*

Fig. 6. An inscription honoring one L. Papius Lupercus, "[of the tribe of] Fal[erna]," probably to be dated to the time of Tiberius. Papius was a colonist (the Falerna were not native to Corinth), and apparently a generous benefactor, to judge from the honorary offices he received—aedile, agonothetes, duovir quinquennalis—usually given in return for gifts or services to the city. The last three lines indicate that "Papia, d[aughter of] L[ucius], wife of Donatus, [and] Methe, [his] grandmother," dedicated the monument—again evidence of the prominence and wealth of at least some Roman women in the colony.

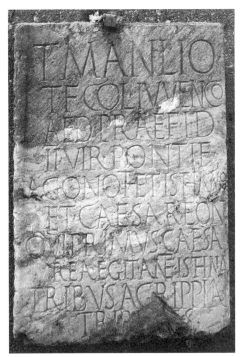

Fig. 7. An inscription honoring Titus Manlius Juvencus, who among other honorific offices was the first to schedule games honoring Caesar before the traditional Isthmian games, probably early in the rule of Augustus and honoring the latter's victory at Actium. That Juvencus is identified in the third line as "praef[ectus] i[ure] d[icundo]" indicates not only his enthusiasm for Roman rule, but apparently a close relationship to the emperor himself; a praefectus iure dicundo was appointed to fulfill the actual responsibilities of duovir on behalf of the emperor, or another important non-Corinthian, whenever the city bestowed the honor of duovir in absentia.

woman being "a deformed male."[11] Man is "hot, fertile, perfectly formed and contributes soul to the generation of a new being; woman is cold, infertile, deformed and contributes the body."[12] In the world of Plato and Aristotle, there is no conception of equality between men and women, between Greeks and barbarians, between masters and slaves.[13] They show no concern for the weak of society. Rather, their philosophy contributes to cementing the structure of the status quo of the Greco-Roman world.

Stoicism developed more systematically to support a ruling, dominant philosophy or an ideology for the dominant culture (the elite ruling class). The Stoics maintained that the cosmos is a unified body bound by the spirit (*pneuma*).[14] The Stoic poet Manilius explains:[15]

> This fabric which forms the body of the boundless universe, together with its members composed of nature's diverse elements, air and fire, earth and level sea, is ruled by the force of a divine spirit; by sacred dispensation the deity brings harmony and governs with hidden purpose, arranging mutual bonds between all parts, so that . . . the whole may stand fast in kinship despite its variety of forms.

Furthermore, differing qualities of the spirit rank everything in the cosmos.[16] The Stoics believed that the world is ordered by reason (*nous*), which "pervades every part of the world . . . Only there is difference of degree; in some parts there is more of it, in others less."[17] In it, the wise should rule the foolish because the wise have *logos*.[18] Notably, the human body was a microcosm, becoming an intrinsic part of the hierarchical cosmos in which body parts run as a "hierarchical chain of command."[19] The Stoics never challenged the status quo of society, based as it was on power, inequality, and on the slavery system, choosing instead to emphasize the ideal of one-world and the unity of human beings. In doing so, they urged political unity and acceptance of "natural" hierarchies in the social body.[20] Tellingly, for Stoics, unity and hierarchy go hand in hand. Furthermore, they avoided the topic of slavery by internalizing or spiritualizing it through the moral quality of life without looking at the experience of the lowly (the marginalized or the oppressed).[21] According to Cicero, slavery is defined as slavery to one's desires: "Or look again at others, petty, narrow-minded men, or confirmed pessimists, or spiteful, envious, ill-tempered creatures, unsociable, abusive, and brutal; others again enslaved to the follies of love, impudent or reckless wanton, headstrong and yet irresolute, always changing their minds."[22] Similarly, Seneca avoids the issue of slavery by emphasizing inner self-control and closing his eyes to the external conditions of life:[23]

It is a mistake for anyone to believe that the condition of slavery penetrates into the whole being of a man. The better part of him is exempt. Only the body is at the mercy and disposition of a master;

Fig. 8. Although Philo mentions a thriving Jewish community in Corinth (Ad Gaium 36), the Jewish community may not have enjoyed great wealth: this Greek inscription, "[syn]agōgē ebr[aiōn]" ("synagogue of the Hebrews"), is roughly carved. (The use of Greek may indicate a date in the second century C.E., since earlier inscriptions were almost all in Latin; or it may indicate the Jewish community's use of Greek.)

but the mind is its own master, and is so free and unshackled that not even this prison of the body, in which it is confined, can restrain it from using its own powers, following mighty aims, and escaping into the infinite to keep the company with the stars. It is, therefore, the body that Fortune hands over to a master; it is this body that he buys, it is this that he sells; that inner part cannot be delivered into bondage. All that issues from this is free; nor, indeed, are we able to command all things from slavery, nor are they compelled to obey us in all things; they will not carry out orders that are hostile to the state, and they will not lend their hands to any crime.

Cicero and Seneca emphasize inner virtues as true moral quality. In this view, slavery is not a moral problem; the problem is each individual's inability to deal with any difficulties whether one is a slave or not.[24] Because of this hierarchical worldview, the Stoics and high culture emphasized the rhetoric of *homonoia* (concord) to the public.[25] The fable of Menenius Agrippa's speech, retold by Livy, a Roman historian in the first century B.C.E., also reveals the ideology of the ruling class.[26] In the fable, the lower body parts (hands, feet, etc.) rebelled against the stomach because the stomach consumes everything without working at all. The point of complaint and rebellion is unfairness or inequality. But the rebelling parts are told to continue to work for the body; otherwise, not only the stomach but the whole body will be destroyed. The rhetoric of the fable emphasizes the hierarchical unity of the social body. But the question is, did this rhetoric of "concord" (or unity) take into account the marginalized or the oppressed? And how did the marginalized respond to it?

Fig. 9. This first-century inscription gives striking evidence of the social status of at least a small part of the Corinthian church. Originally made of Bronze letters set into inscribed limestone, the inscription reads, "Erastus, in return for his aedileship, laid the pavement at his own expense" (s[ua] p[ecunia] stravit). This is almost certainly the Erastus whom Paul greets in Rom. 16:23 as "city administrator" (oikonomos tēs poleōs—a term attested elsewhere as equivalent of the Latin aedile).

In addition, the politics of the hegemonic body appears in examples of the ruling ideologies and political strategies. Augustus's power in the Roman Empire calls for one man's rule, which is supported by an ideology of peace and security that nobody can bring to the empire except through the hegemonic body, whose head is Augustus himself. After the victory of the civil war in 31 B.C.E., Octavius earned from the Senate two important positions, *princeps* and *Augustus*, with a variety of existing positions (consul thirteen times, *pontifex maximus* in 12 B.C.E., tribune for life in 22 B.C.E., and imperator or commander-in-chief).[27] With these various titles, Augustus became the head of the hegemonic body. In fact, Augustus's achievements were recognized through various symbolic acts and literary works. For instance, every military triumph included a great march displaying captured bandits and slaves. In addition, many splendid building projects were also initiated to show

Fig. 10. **Roman power and public space in Corinth.** *The Corinthian theater, originally built at the end of the fifth century B.C.E., was in subsequent centuries the site for public declarations regarding the city's future. In the third century B.C.E., Aratos of Sikyon stood in the theater to declare Corinth's freedom from Macedonian domination; in 196 B.C.E., the Roman general Flamininus announced in the theater that he was withdrawing Roman troops from Greece. (They would return in force, and destroy the city fifty years later.) The Roman colonists later repaired the theater; one prominent Corinthian, Erastus, paid for paving a courtyard just to its east (see Fig. 9). By the early third century C.E., the theater was in use as a Roman arena.*

Fig. 11. A monument "sacred to Victory" shows the prevalence in the Corinthian colony of worship of the Roman goddess.

Fig. 12. The Roman rostra (or bēma: *see Acts 18:12-17), located almost exactly at the center of the Roman Forum. Here Roman officials stood to address the citizens of Corinth, and here, according to Acts, the proconsul Gallio took his seat to hear charges brought against Paul—and to dismiss them as matters of Jewish custom, of no concern to Rome.*

Figs. 13 and 14. Coins of Roman Corinth. The first bears an image of Julius Caesar, who founded the colony, and an inscription with its official name, "Laus Iuli[a] Cor[i] n[thiensis]." The second depicts Livia, wife of Augustus; the reverse portrays a temple with a cult statue and the inscription gent[is] Iuli[ae], "Of the Julian Family." Livia was chief priestess of the cult of the deified Augustus.

Figs. 15 and 16. The most important gods of ancient Corinth—Poseidon and Aphrodite—came to be worshipped in their Latin guises. The first inscription is dedicated by Gnaeus Babbius Philinus as "sacred to Neptune." The second reads [Ve]neri, "To Venus." A temple to Venus was built, or expanded, in the early first century C.E., perhaps indicating a shift away from Aphrodite of the Corinthians to Venus Genetrix, mother of Aeneas—mythic ancestor of Augustus.

Fig. 17. An inscription to "the deified Ju[lius] Caesar." Under the Republic the terms deus *("god") and* divus *("divine") had been almost interchangeable; under Augustus,* divus *came to be reserved for former emperors and their immediate families. When Julius Caesar was declared* divus, *Augustus became* divi filius *("son of God" or "son of the deified [Caesar]").*

Fig. 18. An inscription dedicated by "members of the tribe of Agrippa" to Callicratea, "daughter of Philesius, priestess in perpetuity of the Providence of Augustus and of the security of the people, . . . well-deserving." A priesthood like Callicratea's was an honor granted to men and women of wealth and influence, usually for a limited term; they were chosen for their ability to provide the city with festivals, games, and sacrifices suitable to the celebration of the cult.

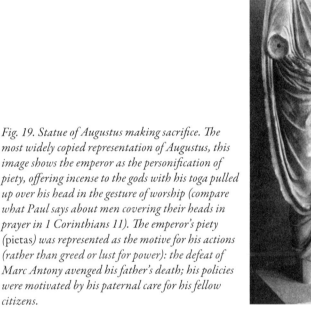

Fig. 19. Statue of Augustus making sacrifice. The most widely copied representation of Augustus, this image shows the emperor as the personification of piety, offering incense to the gods with his toga pulled up over his head in the gesture of worship (compare what Paul says about men covering their heads in prayer in 1 Corinthians 11). The emperor's piety (pietas) was represented as the motive for his actions (rather than greed or lust for power): the defeat of Marc Antony avenged his father's death; his policies were motivated by his paternal care for his fellow citizens.

Augustus's glory and to maintain power. Virgil's *Aeneid* is an ideological product that legitimates the Roman Empire's ideology of peace and security. The Roman way of hierarchical order can bring peace and security, while subjugating all others to this rule.[28] In summary, the politics of the hegemonic body does not consider the voices of the lowly, and its philosophical, ideological basis is in hierarchical dualism, assuring that the low class will serve the high class.

The Body Politic of the Democratic-Inclusive Body

In contrast with the body politic of the hegemonic body, the democratic-inclusive body is voiceless, formless, seemingly silent, docile, and an unorganized body. Postmodern, postcolonial sensitivity brings to the forefront this hidden but real voice in the Greco-Roman world. Indeed, this voice is utterly marginalized; slaves yearn for but have no place to claim their voice for freedom and a universal vision for all human beings. Though no direct evidence exists that the most marginalized spoke against the hegemonic powers, we do have a glimpse through the voice of the Cynics. Diogenes, for example, opposed the politics of the hegemonic body and protested against the dominant discourse and ideology by performing unconventional acts.[29] Unfortunately, scholars usually do not seriously ponder his anti-conventional wisdom and the spirit of protest against the hegemonic body. But in fact, the Cynics taught "in a very public, visible, spectacular, provocative, and sometimes scandalous way of life."[30] The teachings or behaviors of the Cynics draw a strong contrast with the teachings of the hegemonic philosophers such as the Stoics, who from a Cynic point of view emphasized a kind of logo-centrism or mere rhetoric without action. Philosophers in the Platonic, Aristotelian, and Stoic traditions emphasized "a doctrine, text or at least . . . some theoretical principles of their philosophy . . . But now in the Cynic tradition, the main references for the philosophy are not to the texts or doctrines, but to exemplary lives."[31] In other words, the Cynics tried to embody their teachings, challenging the dominant society's hegemonic body. So often, the Cynics used a theater or any public place to draw the attention of the public, thus delivering a radical message of freedom for all. Foucault points out that "Cynic *parrhesia* (free speech or truth-telling) had recourse to scandalous behavior or attitudes which called into question collective habits, opinions, standards of decency, institutional rules."[32] Indeed, Diogenes problematizes the idea of democracy that does not give "equal place to all forms of parrhesia, even the worst."[33] From the resistant, transformative voice of the Cynics, one can say that the Cynics envisioned a bigger community for "all" that included slaves. One can find such a hope from Diogenes of Sinope (404–323 B.C.E. who when "asked where he came from, he replied, 'I am a citizen of the world.'"[34] This is indeed a different kind of cosmopolitanism, nothing like the hegemonic, hierarchical body politic of concord. Rather, it promotes undiscriminating care and rights for all.

Paul and the Democratic-Inclusive Body

How does Paul intersect with the conflicting voices in the Greco-Roman and/or the Jewish world? Whose voice does Paul represent, the hegemonic or the marginalized voice? According to some scholars who use socio-rhetorical methods, Paul is an ideal Stoic man, concerned about concord (*homonoia*). In this view, Paul does not challenge hierarchical, patriarchal society. But from a perspective attentive to "voices from the margins," we can read Paul as a different voice, a voice proclaiming Christ crucified (1 Corinthians 1–4), as we see similarly in the Cynic philosopher's (Diogenes of Sinope) anti-conventional acts and *parrhēsia* (free speech or "truth telling"). Moreover, as Laurence Welborn suggests, Paul's talk of playing the role of the fool identified him with the grassroots (slaves).[35] As Diogenes deconstructs the conventional wisdom of social, hierarchical unity, so Paul's preaching of Christ crucified also plays a role in deconstructing the conventional wisdom of power, honor, and hierarchical unity. Paul also embodies all his teachings in his life, radically identifying with Christ crucified; he carries in his body the death of Jesus (2 Cor 4:10; Gal 6:17). How could Paul overlook the crucifixion of slaves and Jews while preaching Christ crucified? Ancient descriptions of crucifixion of slaves defy equanimity, as when Varro mentions the "rotting corpses" of the crucified:[36]

> If this moisture is in the ground no matter how far down, in a place from which it *pote* 'can' be taken, it is a *puteus* 'well' (or pit); . . . From *putei* 'wells' comes the town name, such as *Puteoli*, because around this place there are many hot and cold spring-waters; unless rather from *putor* 'stench,' because the place is often *putidus* 'stinking' with smells of sulphur and alum. Outside the town there are *puticuli* 'little pits,' named from *putei* 'pits'; because there are the people used to be buried in *putei* 'pits'; unless rather, as Aelius writes, the *puticuli* are so called because the corpses which had been thrown out *putescebant* 'used to rot' there, in the public burial-place which is beyond the Esquiline.

Horace also speaks of the "whitened bones" of the crucified:[37]

> How can I recount in gory detail how those shades, exchanging words with Sagana, set all that dismal space echoing with their melancholy grating voices? And how those two stealthily buried in the ground a wolf's beard and the tooth of a spotted snake? And how the flames sputtered and soared when the wax puppet was burned? . . . How you would have laughed and taken delight in seeing Canidia's

teeth and Sagana's high-piled wig spilling to the ground together with their magic herbs and love-knots—all that necromancy dropping from their arms.

Juvenal speaks of the morsels of flesh of the crucified which the carrion birds plucked from the crosses to feed their young.[38] The Roman novelist Chariton also records a vivid description of the crucifixion of a group of slaves:[39]

> They were discovered and all securely fastened in the stocks for the night, and when day came the estate manager told Mithridates what had happened. Without even seeing them or listening to their defense he immediately ordered the sixteen cell-mates to be crucified. They were duly brought out, chained together at foot and neck, each carrying his own cross. The executioners added this grim public spectacle to the requisite penalty as a deterrent to others so minded.

In fact, the experience of the cross in the Greco-Roman world cannot be spiritualized, as we can infer from the Roman comic poet Plautus's works, in which contents of the plays are reflections of real people.[40] Those plays depict real, shameful experiences of members from the lower class in the Roman world, who were often killed and mistreated, made naked and treated as invisible. The account of the crucifixion of the runaway slave in the "Laureolus" mime illustrates a bizarre scene of crucifixion:

> In a farce called "Laureolus," in which the chief actor falls as he is making his escape and vomits blood, several understudies so vied with one another in giving evidence of their proficiency that the stage swam in blood. A nocturnal performance besides was rehearsing, in which scenes from the lower world were represented by Egyptians and Aethiopians.

For the elite, the plays are a source of humor because they are not like those tragic characters; however, the lowest people may shed tears because they are like the characters in the play.

The crucifixion of Jews also is recorded by Josephus and Philo. Josephus testifies that the Sadducean high priest, Alexander Janneus (in office 103–76 B.C.E.), crucified eight hundred Pharisees while their wives and children were slaughtered before their eyes as they were hung and dying.[41] Josephus also witnesses crucifixion during Titus's siege of Jerusalem, calling it "the most wretched of deaths."[42] Philo records the scene of crucifixion when at the time of Caligula (37–41 C.E.) a number of Jews were tortured and crucified in the amphitheater of Alexandria to entertain the people:[43]

> But this man did not order men who had already perished on crosses to be taken down, but he commanded living men to be crucified, men to whom the very time itself gave, if not entire forgiveness, still, at all events, a brief and temporary respite from punishment; and he did this after they had been beaten by scourgings in the middle of the theatre; and after he had tortured them with fire and sword; and the spectacle of their sufferings was divided; for the first part of the exhibition lasted from the morning to the third or fourth hour, in which the Jews were scourged, were hung up, were tortured on the wheel, were condemned, and were dragged to execution through the middle of the orchestra; and after this beautiful exhibition came the dancers, and the buffoons, and the flute-players, and all the other diversions of the theatrical contests.

The Roman historian Tacitus also records the brutal crucifixion of Christians during Nero's time: "[M]ockery of every sort was added to their deaths. Covered with the skins of wild beasts, they were torn to death by dogs. Or they were fastened on crosses and, when daylight faded, were burned to serve as lamps by night."[44]

I cite these passages to press the point: How could we believe that Paul would disregard the experiences of the most vulnerable, the slaves and victims of the Empire, when he talks about Christ crucified? How could we believe that the same Paul who made the cross central to his message would side with the hegemonic body politic based on the Stoic ideal of unity? It appears, to the contrary, that the image of Christ crucified deconstructs society's wisdom, power, and glory.

If we understand Paul against the backdrop of the larger Greco-Roman and Jewish world, we may understand what he says in 2 Corinthians in a new light: "For in him every one of God's promises is a 'Yes.'" It is a *yes* to life in the world. It means that all destructive forms of oppression in society should be stopped through the re-envisioning of an alternative community for all (society), based on love, sacrifice, and others-centered "community" ethics. Paul seems confident about this call of yes-to-life: "Yes, everything is for your sake, so that grace, as it extends to more and more people, may increase thanksgiving, to the glory of God" (2 Cor 4:15). In this view, Paul can be read as presenting an alternative worldview that there is no slave or free "in Christ"; all are free and children of God. God says yes to life in the midst of deathlike hopelessness in the world. God's affirming of life is yes to all people.

These considerations suggest that we align Paul with the voices of marginality and diversity in his world. It is misleading to view Paul as a social conservative who cares only for his own community or as a Hellenized person with an ideal of unity in Christ at the expense of social diversity.[45] An older view of Paul as a social conservative does not consider Paul's worldview or ethics in their entirety,[46] making him only a triumphant, systematic theologian or the great founder of Christianity. But Paul's theology and ethics on behalf of the downtrodden involves a radical theology of the cross.[47] In that regard, we can understand his exchange with the community at Corinth in terms of his envisioning a new world of Christic embodiment.[48] The next step is to see how Paul carried forward this vision in his response to the Corinthians' issues.

———— The "Disembodiment" of Christ in Corinth ————

Now in the Corinthian community we can think of the *disembodiment* of the *Christic body,* because some members of the community do not live up to Christ's life and death. Namely, disembodiment occurs simply because they do not live out Christ's body, a phrase best understood as an attributive genitive—thus "Christic body" (compare "body of sin" = "sinful body" in Rom 6:6.) The result of this disembodiment is expressed in various issues and conflicts in the letter: divisions (1:12), sexual immorality (chaps. 5–6), marriage-related matters (7:1), eating of meat sacrificed to idols (chaps. 8, 10), the rights of Paul (chap. 9), women's head coverings (11:1-16), the Lord's Supper (11:17-34), and resurrection (chap. 15). All of these issues involve an *ideological conflict* within the community.[49] We may attribute a hegemonic ideology to a segment of the community that we may characterize variously, for example, from a socioeconomic perspective as representatives of the upper class, or in terms of spiritual proclivity, as enthusiasts, a party of the "royal Christ," or ethically as libertines.[50] The strong or powerful construct their worldview based on a social conservatism that is the ideal of unity and hierarchy, as we see in the case of Stoicism and its drive for the unity of the social body. In fact, in 1 Corinthians 15 we can hear the voice of the marginalized, though indirectly, through the hegemonic voice, because the existence of the oppressive voice indicates the existence of others as the objects of oppression. The masculine hegemonic voice that silences women means that some women were not silent, quite possibly because of their egalitarian voice, as Antoinette Clark Wire has suggested regarding the activity of women prophets in the community. Similar issues obtain with regard to eating food sacrificed to idols.

Therefore, it is urgent to see how Paul responds to this hegemonic voice or ideology that has occasioned disembodiment of the Christic body. The failures of some Corinthians have to do with their not living according to the image or the role of Christ crucified (1 Cor 2:2). That is why there is great dysfunction of the *ekklēsia,* which requires the living-out of the *Christic body.* The manifestations of this disembodiment are not a series of isolated specific issues, but symptoms of an ideology that involves all aspects of their life. The life of the Christic body is central to Paul's response, which necessarily then involves a critique of the disembodiment of Christ on the part of the Corinthian elite. This understanding is different from that of Sandra Polaski and Elizabeth Castelli, for example, who consider Paul's response a matter of asserting his own revelatory power or authority. [51]

Divisions

How to understand the factions mentioned in 1:12 is critical to our understanding of the Corinthian community. Some scholars conclude that there are only three factions (Paul's, Apollos's, and Cephas's) without counting Christ's faction as a possible cause of divisions.[52] The general interpretive practice has assumed that "I belong to Christ" (1:13) was offered as a way to unify the church into a community in which members have the same mind and judgment.[53] However, there are some problems with that conclusion, as David Odell-Scott points out.[54] The Greek verb *memeristai*[55] can be either a middle or a passive voice ("Has Christ distributed himself?"

versus "Has Christ been divided?"). In view of the logical connection between 1:12 and 1:13, we may expect negative rhetorical questions for all factions mentioned in 1:13. Namely, "Has Christ distributed himself?" (No!) "Was Paul crucified for you?" (No!) "Were you baptized in the name of Paul?" (No!) "In this way, the first negative rhetorical question becomes a critique of the fourth self-declaration ('I belong to Christ')."[56] There, too, the answer is "No!" Nobody can exercise theocratic power by calling on the authority of Christ. Nobody represents Christ. What is essential is to boast of Christ crucified. Therefore, the traditional translation, "Has Christ been divided?" (1:13), is not the only possible one. The other possibility (middle voice)—"Has Christ distributed himself?"—is probable when one recognizes that Christ is not equated with the church or the community. (Such ideas come only in later Deutero-Pauline letters!)[57] Therefore, it would seem more helpful, exegetically and theologically, to think of *four* factions, including the Christ party, which seek to exercise "theocratic" power in the community. Thus, certainly, the principal cause of the Corinthian conflict should include the Christ party, which seeks to reinforce hegemonic power based on some combination of birth, region, tradition, and patriarchy.[58]

Paul's response to the hegemonic voice is to reverse the conventional wisdom that overpowers "others" by proclaiming Christ crucified, which is a folly and nonsense to the "powerful" hegemonic body (1:10–4:21). Therefore, we should not read 1:10 ("you be united in the same mind and the same purpose") as a thesis statement for 1 Corinthians. The problem in the community is not a lack of "unity" but an overpowering, hegemonic ideology of "power" over the weak and against the voice of women's freedom and equality. In the end, the problem is not, in the Stoic sense, a lack of "unity" (concord) which does not allow differences or diversity, but a lack of respect.

Sexual Immorality

Among the interpretations of the sexual immorality described in 5:1-13 and 6:9-20, Hans Conzelmann's view stands out because of the clarity of his language regarding the community boundary. According to him, keeping the purity of the body is a duty for a person belonging to Christ, because there is a real connection between members (*melē*) and

Christ.[59] So members of Christ should keep the body from fornication: "to have extramarital sexual intercourse is to repudiate the relationship of belonging to the 'body of Christ.'"[60] Similarly, the social-science or socio-rhetorical reading also emphasizes the boundary of the community against the pagan world. According to Mitchell, "the insiders are *melē christou,* but the prostitute is clearly not (6:15) . . . She is *beyond the boundary* and is indeed a threat to the health of the whole community."[61] Thus, unity means fending off sexual immorality. Similarly, Neyrey views fornication as pollution; what is necessary is to control the body boundary in such a way as to maintain a pure body.[62]

But Käsemann interprets the issue of sexual immorality differently. That is, he emphasizes Christian ethics in terms of the lordship of Christ, which involves the "corporeality of human life, organic to the creation, claimed by God as his own right, yet threatened by the cosmic power."[63] Becoming one body (*hen sōma*) with the prostitute or the Christ (6:16-17) is a matter of service; Christians enter "the realm into which we are incorporated with our bodies and to which we are called to render service in the body, that is, total service; service that embraces all our different relationships in and to the world."[64]

Although Käsemann's reading is similar to mine in terms of his emphasis on the "relational" language of body as a living space, my reading specifically connects sexual immorality to power conflicts in which some people exercise their freedom irresponsibly at the expense of the whole community. This power conflict echoes a Corinthian slogan that "all things are lawful" (6:12; 10:23)—an example of excessive individualism[65] by which sexually immoral people do harm to the community, the majority of whom live vulnerably on the margin of society with little or no protection.

Marriage-Related Matters

A Corinthian slogan[66] in 7:1 ("it is well for a man not to touch a woman") is ample evidence that there are some people who consider asceticism as a hegemonic power that is used to control the household, the community, and society, as Brown suggests in his book *Body and Society.*[67] But Paul corrects the view of this hegemonic, hierarchical relationship between husband and wife and elevates the sanctity of marriage in serving the God of the community and love (7:14, 32-35).[68] In this perspective, Paul can be read as supporting interdependent marriage relationships, which challenge the hegemonic, ascetic practice of the Greco-Roman world, as well as that of the Corinthian community, because a healthy marriage relationship is unconcerned with who has power but how the couple serve each other (interdependent relationship). Thus, Paul declares that just as the Corinthians "were bought with a price" (7:23), so everything that they do, every step they take, and every breath they breathe, must be related to sanctifying God, who requires holistic living, which relates to the transformation and redemption of the world. As Christ's body of sanctity, the Corinthians should not become "slaves of human masters" (7:23); instead, "in whatever condition you were called, there remain with God" (7:24). Therefore, what they must do is to "remain with God" under any circumstances (7:17-24). "Remaining with God" is not a passive mode of doing nothing, but it can be understood positively; the Corinthians should stay with *God's initiative*—God's power that passes beyond human ideology and power. In this way, Paul can be read as challenging social conservatism and nullifying human constructions of power. "Remain with God" implies "see what God is doing." Braxton also reads this positive message of remaining with God, viewing ambiguity in the text as "an intrinsic feature of the text" that allows for challenging slavery; 7:22a ("called in the Lord") can be read to affirm the essential ministry of justice.[69]

Eating Meat Sacrificed to Idols

Regarding the eating of meat sacrificed to idols and eating in an idol temple (8:1-13), we see the conflict between those who have "knowledge" of freedom ("all things are lawful") and those who have weak consciences. Paul says such "knowledge puffs up; but love builds up" (8:1). A necessary knowledge is to care for others: "take care that this liberty of yours does not somehow become a stumbling block to the weak" (8:9). Therefore, God will recognize such a person who recognizes others (8:2-3). Otherwise, the consequence will be great; not caring for the weak is the same as sinning against Christ (8:12). It is striking, indeed, that the weak and the strong should live together, respecting each other in a beloved community for all. Identification of Christ with those weak members is a sign that there is no complete community if anyone is excluded. From this holistic point of view, members should live with respectful differences between knowledge and conscience. The hegemonic voice of "objective" knowledge cannot exist at the expense of "others." God knows those who live with this kind of sensitivity to the existence of "others" (8:3). One can see here a community spirit: "If food is a cause of their falling, I will never eat meat, so that I may not cause one of them to fall" (8:13). From this community perspective, freedom can be sacrificed for others (8:24). Likewise, Paul becomes a slave to all by giving up his rights (9:19-23).

As seen previously, the urgent issues in 8:1-13 turn to the question of how to deal with "others" (10:1-33).[70] As opposed to the traditional understanding of this text (chs. 8, 10), as it is read as a cultural, theological boundary ("flee from the worship of idols" in 10:14), what is at stake is not a mere denial of other religions or cultures. Rather, the problem arises due to "participation" with demons (10:20), for example, participating in destructive, hegemonic practices in paganism and in the community. The issue here is more than whether members of the community eat food offered to idols; it has to do with being sensitive to each other without causing others to fall. For this, the Corinthians "were called into *the fellowship* of his Son, Jesus Christ our Lord" (1:9). Accordingly, on the basis of fellowship with Christ, members of the community should not be hostile toward others: "give no offense to Jews or to Greeks or to the assembly of God." What is most important is, "so, whether you eat or drink, or whatever you do, do everything for the glory of God" (10:32). For this goal, Paul turns to the spirit of the community by declaring: "just as I try to please everyone in everything I do, not seeking my own advantage, but that of many, so that they may be saved" (10:33).

Rights of Paul

Some scholars see chapter 9 as a "digression"[71] or an "interruption"[72] because chapter 9 seems to discontinue the topic of chapter 8 (food offered to idols). Chapter 9 deals with Paul's defense of his apostleship.[73] However, as I noted in my discussion about the food offered to idols, the conflicting power context of chapter 8 (between the strong and the weak) seems to continue in chapter 9 as well, because Paul's emphasis on the "free gospel" of Christ (9:12, 18) advocates for freedom of all people—especially for those excluded from the Roman system of patronage.[74] Paul clarifies that he is called to make the gospel available for all by becoming "a slave to all" (9:19) and "all things to all people" (9:22). Actually, Paul's mention of the *free gospel* (9:18) can be understood against the backdrop of a patronage system because his rejection of money from the community can mean his own social death.[75] But Paul dares to do so, even in the face of this oppressive patronage system, as Ched Myers observes:[76]

> Paul, however, recognized patronage as the glue that held in place all the oppressive relationships of the empire. Following the Christ who had been executed by that empire, Paul instead embraced the status of a "slave" (the lowest social class), in order that he might serve all people equally, unbeholden to those of high political or economic standing (1 Cor 9:18-23) . . . It was expected that Paul would support his pastoral ministry in Corinth by positioning himself as an "in-house philosopher" sponsored by a wealthy patron. Paul, however, refused to become a client of the rich. Instead, he insisted instead on supporting himself through a trade (1 Cor 9; see 1 Thess 2:9). For this he was severely criticized by the Corinthian aristocracy, both for offending the patron class and for lowering his prestige by working with his hands.

The possibility of Paul's rejection of the patronage system does not receive due attention frequently, as it is shadowed by the view of Paul's *individual* piety. For example, C. K. Barrett credits Paul with being a great theologian because Paul gives up all, not boasting of what he did. Similarly, Sandra Polaski reads 9:3-18 as Paul's voluntary renunciation of rights to emphasize Paul's authority and power.[77] But from the perspective of marginality in which the voice of the downtrodden is heard, Paul's rejection of financial support from the community can be read as a protest against the hegemonic voice in the community.[78]

From this perspective, Paul's free, independent spirit coincides with the free gospel of Christ for all. His opposition to the client system is clear in 9:15-22, in which he emphasizes that the gospel is "free" to all (9:18); it cannot become a weapon to control, discriminate against, or exclude others. To demonstrate the power of "the gospel of Christ" (9:12) as such, Paul adapts himself to all living conditions (9:19-22), by being "under the law" (v. 20) or "outside the law" (v. 21). Indeed, his bold statements in 9:15-22 resoundingly resist the patron-client system and the hegemonic voice in the community. In addition, with this line of thought of "independence" and a binding love for all, Paul relinquishes those apostolic rights mentioned in 9:4-14.[79]

Women's Head Coverings

Regarding disputes over women's head coverings (11:1-16), most scholarly exegesis converges around no fewer than five interpretive possibilities:[80]

1. Paul wants to limit women's hairstyles because he is concerned about the confusion of gender difference in Corinth.[81]
2. Paul is following the social convention of hierarchy or unequal relationship (so women's change of head covering is considered a radical disobedience to the social convention).[82]
3. Paul seeks to limit such practices due to some disturbing acts by women at worship.[83]
4. It is not Paul's own voice but an interpolation by later editors.[84]
5. Paul quotes the hegemonic, patriarchal voice of the opponents (11:4-7) to counter it.[85]

Though each position has merit, the last position sounds viable and consistent with Paul's overall theology in his letter.[86] The exegetical, literary clue to making this option plausible comes from v. 11, *"nevertheless, in the Lord woman is not independent of man or man independent of woman. . . . but all things come from God"* (11:11-12). Paul deconstructs his opponents' gender hierarchy (7:9) through God's power. In v. 16, Paul confirms that there is no such custom to regulate head coverings or gender relations apart from God. God's initiative nullifies all human construction of power based on gender hierarchy.

The Lord's Supper

There is more complexity in the interpretation of the Lord's Supper (11:17-34) than normally is thought. These complexities range from economic to ideological conflicts. Given a cultural, social atmosphere of table fellowship, the host is usually powerful and honored as benefactor.[87]

Likewise, the Lord's Supper might be such an occasion for a social, religious gathering.[88] Understandably, those who can afford to come early are the rich, whereas the poor come late or do not attend at all for unknown reasons.[89] According to Theissen, the problem in this Lord's Supper is that the rich behave improperly by not waiting for others to join them. In other words, Theissen's reading of the community in Corinth is based on the idea of social functionalism ("love patriarchalism"), accepting the status quo of society and the community.[90]

But Theissen's view raises some concerns for me. There are two options for understanding Paul's position regarding the Lord's Supper:

1. Paul accepts the role of the rich in the community and teaches a "love patriarchalism" (the "functionalist" or "conservative" reading); or
2. It is not Paul, but the rich who seek to practice this "love patriarchalism": Paul's own view could be described as non-conformist compared to that of the rich.

Understanding the vitality of the Christic body in Paul's response points us to the second option. We recognize the radicality of Paul's theology once we take into account that his metaphor of the "body of Christ" is a metaphor of *living Christ crucified*. It deconstructs the ideologies of the powers and reconstructs the community (*ekklēsia*) through Christic embodiment. Seen in this way, Paul critiques the "powerful" (not the rich only) who subordinate others under certain ideologies, whether protognostic (ascetic) or libertine (licentious).[91] By analogy to the modern experience of the church today, it is probable that people in the same faction sit together around the table, sharing their food with in-group members. For whatever reason, Paul is concerned about the hegemonic voices in the community as we see in 1:12.

Resurrection

Some Corinthians who deny the "resurrection of the dead" (15:12) could have been enthusiasts who claim that they live resurrection in the present.[92] The Sophia tradition could be responsible for this denial of the resurrection of the dead because they (of the Sophia tradition) live the time of resurrection now in the way that they know the heavenly truth or life.[93] These people ask rhetorically, "How are the dead raised? In what kind of *body* do they come?" (1 Cor 15:35). Paul answers: "Fool! What you sow does not come to life unless it dies" (15:36). For Paul, dying every day (15:31) is to accept sacrifice for others. For Paul, "dying" seems to be an association with Christ crucified, as we see in the "body of Christ" as Christ's body given out for many at the institution of the Lord's Supper (11:23-26). Likewise, Paul seems to locate the human problem in the "denial of death,"[94] in the sense that they want to maintain their *fleshly* life forever. This selfish, fleshly desire seeks a body that does not die with their desires. Those who ask sarcastically, "With what kind of body do they come?" are eager to prolong their earthly, hegemonic power. To oppose the power language based on earthly, physical body (*sōma psychikon*), Paul coins a new phrase, "a spiritual body" (*sōma pneumatikon*) (15:44), which is oxymoronic and nonsensical to the ears of Greeks because spirit and body (or flesh) cannot go together. As is clear, the point of Paul's discourse here is not to describe the status of the resurrection as such, but to reject the human construction of power based on the idea of the fleshly resurrection in terms of holding to power/desires. In this regard, Paul's theology of resurrection exhibits a deconstructive power against those who seek "powers" or prolong their "living" at the expense of others.

Summary

I have analyzed the Corinthian issues from the perspective of power conflicts and suggested that the possible cause of these conflicts is the disposition of elite members of the Corinthian church not to live in a Christic body, but to dominate others. Paul's urgent concern is to construct a community of "all," but not in the sense of the Stoic "unity" or "universal humanity" at the cost of diversity. In this interpretation, Paul's solution is very different from the one that the world provides. The problems in the Corinthian situation have to do with the disembodiment of the Christic body.

CHAPTER FIVE

The Life of the "Body of Christ" in 1 Corinthians

From the outset, we must distinguish the use of the "body of Christ" metaphor in Paul's undisputed letters, especially 1 Cor 12:27 and Rom 12:5, from that in the Deutero-Pauline letters (i.e., Eph 4:12; Col 1:18). In the Deutero-Pauline letters, the phrase refers to an ecclesiological reality and a hierarchical one: the "body of Christ" is ruled by Christ, its "head" (Eph 1:22-23; Col 1:18). In Paul's own letters, on the other hand, the "body of Christ" is associated, by analogy, to Jesus' physical body, and metaphorically, to those who "*live* Christ" or live "in Christ" (*en christō*). Paul directly relates Christ to a metaphor for a way of living in Phil 1:21 ("For to me, living is Christ and dying is gain"), Gal 2:20 ("it is no longer I who live, but it is Christ who lives in me"), and in Gal 2:19 ("I have been crucified with Christ"). The phrases *en christō* or *en christō Iēsou*, repeatedly found in Paul's undisputed letters, also refer to a way of living.[1] Paul expresses the same thought when he speaks of "living for God in Christ Jesus" (*zōntas de tō theō en christō Iēsou*, Rom 6:11). "You are God's temple" (1 Cor 3:16), and "you are a new creation" (2 Cor 5:17) are similar metaphorical phrases. In the undisputed letters, Paul declares the community *is* the "body of Christ" (using the predicate nominative). In the Deutero-Pauline letters[2] (Eph 4:12, Col 1:18), by contrast, the "body of Christ" is the object of the community's action, for example as the community is exhorted "to build the body of Christ" (*eis oikodomēn tou somatos tou christou*, Eph 4:12). In the Deutero-Pauline letters, the metaphor of the "body of Christ" as the church is no longer a metaphor for a way of life, but functions as a metaphor for something "built" (an *oikodomē*), an institution metaphorized as a sort of organic whole.

In the light of the sense of "living" Christ or "living in Christ," the metaphor in 1 Cor 12:27, "you are the body of Christ," can be understood as a reference to Christ's own body in the sense that believers (Corinthians) are called to participate in that body *by living like Christ.* As we shall see, the various ways Paul speaks of the "body of Christ" in 1 Corinthians give us insights into Paul's concerns about the life of the "body" in the Corinthian community.

——— Language for "the Body" in 1 Corinthians ———

Various terms for "body" appear in 1 Corinthians, and these terms are used in different ways. My chief interest is in the use of body language to designate the physical body and especially in Paul's figural speech designating the body, described holistically, as the site of dedication, commitment, or obedience.[3]

First, Paul speaks clearly of the physical, fleshly body in several passages (1 Cor 5:3-5; 13:3; 15:37-38, 44) where his meaning is nonetheless debatable.[4] Scholars read "body" (*sōma*) and "flesh" (*sarx*) in 1 Cor 5:3-5 in a literal sense, so "the destruction of the flesh" (1 Cor 5:5) means physical death. Hans Conzelmann goes one step further in understanding the destruction of the flesh as the result of thrusting someone "out of the body of Christ into the realm of wrath."[5] Remember, however, that unity achieved through the expulsion of members is a forced unity, as practiced by the Roman world, and therefore *cannot* have been Paul's meaning. The destruction of the flesh can also be understood in a figurative way, as the destruction of fleshly desires, self-seeking pleasure, or dominating power rather than as the destruction of the physical body itself. Paul may not be suggesting that expulsion of an offender is the solution to a problem in the Corinthian church; rather, the solution may be to put to death the deeds of the flesh. Paul speaks figuratively of the destruction of the body as a way of denouncing sexual immorality, "so that (the offender's) spirit may be saved" (1 Cor 5:5).

Second, Paul speaks of the body in a holistic way, incompatible with any division or any entanglement with another body that would jeopardize its integrity, in 1 Cor 6:13 (the body is for the Lord), 6:15-18 (the body must not be made the "members" of a prostitute), 6:19 (the body is a temple of the Spirit), 6:20 (glorify God in your body), 7:34 (whole commitment renders the body holy), and 12:27 (where the members are united as the "body of Christ").[6] Conzelmann understands the holistic body in terms of maintaining holiness: "to have extramarital sexual intercourse is to repudiate the relationship of belonging to the 'body of Christ.'"[7] He also interprets the "members (*melē*) of Christ" (1 Cor 6:15) as a real connection with Christ.[8] In this sense, outsiders (prostitutes) are never part of the "body of Christ" and are "a threat to the health of the whole community."[9] However, the phrase *members of Christ* need not be read as referring only to the boundary of the community: it can also be understood as a reference to living like Christ in a holistic, total commitment to the Lord. Thus, being "members of Christ" involves honoring those who are weak, poor, oppressed, and marginalized in the community. In this view, *kollaomai* ("to unite, join, stick to") in 1 Cor 6:16-17 can be understood as a metaphor for living, used to reinforce the sense of total commitment. In this view, 1 Cor 6:13, 15-20, and 7:34 do not speak about a two-step ethics according to which "membership" of the body (the community) is primary, and keeping their individual bodies holy is required as a consequence of membership (so that the prostitute is simply an object of exclusion). Rather, being "members of Christ" is a matter of how individuals live; exclusion of the other is not the point of the metaphor. From this perspective, the issue is not a lack of unity or disciplinary rules but a lack of total commitment to living like Christ as *members* of Christ.

Paul's statement that "you are the body of Christ" in 1 Cor 12:27 also can be understood in terms of the holistic, dedicated body.[10] Actually, 1 Corinthians itself distinguishes between the "body of Christ" (1 Cor 12:27, for example) and the *ekklēsia* (1 Cor 14:4), which is being built as an organic institution.[11] In 1 Cor 12:27, the "body of Christ" (which does not have the definite article in Greek), alluding to the life and death of Christ is a predicate nominative: "you are *body of Christ*" in the sense that as a "Christic body" you are to live like Christ. That is, "you" and the "body of Christ" are one; for "you" (as Christian believers), living is being the "body of Christ." Paul's point is to exhort his hearers to live like Christ. In this way, we might take the genitive "body *of Christ*" as an attributive genitive (which I represent with the phrase *christic* body), not a possessive genitive (i.e., the body *belonging to Christ*).[12] Compare Rom 6:6, when "body of sin" is read as an attributive genitive: "sinful body." As we will see, "you are body of Christ" becomes a central expression of Paul's theology of the cross, his ethics of radical participation in Christ's death, and his hermeneutics of chosen marginality.

An Ethic of the Christic Body

One implication of this way of reading the phrase is that we recognize Paul's primary concerns relate to power conflicts, where what is at stake is "living" as the Christic body rather than maintaining the group as an organism. How to live out the gospel of Christ *with the body* is a central key concern of Paul's theology and ethics.[13] The Corinthian context requires *reconciliation*—not first unity—but reconciliation, made possible only through living like Christ. The hope held out is not a mere asceticism appropriate to identify or distinguish the members of a group, but to give one's body to God through a holistic commitment. The focus on the body as a site of "living" in Christ is much clearer when the body is related to the "living" of the "Christic body" (as I interpret 12:27).

Reading Pauline theology and ethics through metaphors of "living" rather than of "belonging" results in a one-step ethics, in contrast to the usual construal of tension between indicative and imperative in Paul's thought. Individuals must realize the "body of Christ" in their bodies by imitating Christ's self-giving love and sacrifice.[14] This kind of one-step ethical view challenges the view of most exegetical commentators who view Rom 12:1, for example, as an ethical exhortation, the result of faith "in Christ" (Rom 3:21-26). In my interpretation, Paul's theology and ethics cannot be separated from each other. The point is much clearer in First Corinthians, where Paul deconstructs human wisdom and power (1 Corinthians 1–4) and reconstructs the community through the living of the Christic body.

In contrast, the theological or ethical view in the Deutero-Pauline letters is based on the metaphor of membership in a social body, whose head as Christ is "the beginning" (Col 1:18; similarly, Eph 1:22-23). From this "high" christological view, the husband is the head of the wife, just as Christ is to the church in a hegemonic body politic. The Deutero-Pauline letters espouse a universal deontological ethics according to which all people must follow the rules or an authority. This worldview calls for following Christian norms, which tend to be formalized in theocracy or hierarchy. There is no sense of diversity or of the embodiment of obedience found in dying with Christ. Rather, here, Christ died "once and for all," as in a forensic interpretation of salvation according to which an *individual* righteousness is made possible by faith; God as a judge declares that sinners are not guilty and declared righteous once and for all. In fact, many scholars read Paul holding to just such a theology. The implication is that "since you belong to this community, you have to do your duty." There is also a strong boundary drawn between members of the community and the rest of the world. There is no sense of protest or resistance against the hierarchical system itself. (See the summary of these contrasts in Table 1)

Table 1. Comparing Pauline and Deutero-Pauline Uses of the Body Metaphor

	Pauline letters	**Deutero-Pauline letters**
Metaphor of body	Embodiment of Christ	Ecclesiological organism (social body)
View of body	Holistic	Dualistic (inside v. outside)
Body politic	More democratic-inclusive	More hegemonic (hierarchy)
Gender relationships	Mutual dependency	Patriarchy
Ethics	One-step (embodiment)	Two-step (indicative-imperative)
Boundary	Potentially open and embracing	Inflexible and exclusive

Tracing the Christic Body in 1 Corinthians

In the preceding analysis of Paul's use of the term "body" in 1 Corinthians, I suggested that Paul's use of the metaphor involves an ethical exhortation to the community in conflict. Now I turn to the use of the figure *body of Christ* in 1 Corinthians to examine how Paul's use of this figure strengthens the notion of the Christic body.

This figure, like all figures, involves a twofold investment of meaning, because it brings together the (expected) views of the audience and the different views of the author as enunciator, and thus transforms the audience's views. This twofold semantic investment is easy to recognize in the case of a metaphor, which is a particular kind of figure employed to explicate two semantic fields, as Daniel Patte shows, relying on Paul Ricoeur and A. Greimas.[15] For instance, to speak metaphorically of war as a game of chess is to bring together the semantic fields of actual war and of a game in such a way as to posit that they have something in common, a common semantic feature that is actually transformed by the discourse in which the metaphor is used.

The figure at the very center of Paul's discourse in First Corinthians, "the body of Christ," brings together two semantic fields in such a way as to transform the views of his audience. In order to do this, Paul must first speak in a way that will make sense for his interlocutors by rhetorically allowing them to speak; he gives them voice. Then, progressively, Paul transforms their view of the topics at hand by introducing other voices, until he reaches the end of his discourse where he can at last present these topics *in the different way in which he wants his interlocutors to understand them.* This recognition that there are several voices in the text, several view points, is essential for my purpose, since it allows us to hear the voices of people who have been silenced by attributing everything to a single voice, Paul's.

This multifold "semantic discursive structure" of a discourse—in this case, 1 Corinthians—can be recognized in a first approximation by attending to what Patte (following Greimas and others) calls "inverted parallelisms." An inverted parallelism consists of the presentation of a topic from one perspective (the addressees') at the beginning of a discursive unit, and at the end of this unit, the presentation of the same topic (parallelism) from a different, *inverted* perspective.[16] In what follows I will summarize and explain the overall discursive structure of 1 Corinthians. Then, looking more closely at the main features of this discursive structure of 1 Corinthians, I will examine the way in which Paul constructs the figure of the "body of Christ" in 1 Corinthians. This analysis will then allow me to clarify aspects of Paul's theology and ethics that may otherwise be invisible and ignored. The centrality of Christic embodiment, perceived from the perspective of the marginalized, is rooted in the text of 1 Corinthians as a discourse seeking to address power conflicts in Corinth.

As we saw in chapters 1–3, current readings of the "body of Christ" in 1 Corinthians differ depending on the contextual, theological, and analytical choices made by interpreters. For example, the socio-rhetorical tradition (represented by Margaret Mitchell) chooses as its hermeneutical key the concept of unity, which stems directly from the rhetoric of the Greco-Roman upper class. In that view, the problem that Paul faced in Corinth was caused by "division" and solved by "unity."[17] In contrast to similar views, *I read "diversity" as Paul's proposed solution* to power conflicts[18] brought about by an exclusive, hierarchical view of the community as the "body of Christ." In my view, this power conflict comes from different sites in the community and from outside of it as well. Analyzing the figures that Paul constructs in the discursive structure of the letter reveals that the call to be the body of Christ is a call to live Christ crucified (and thus to emulate Paul in his imitation of Christ: 1 Cor 11:1). To be the body of Christ is to live out the Christic body; this requires the death of human wisdom, meaning the death of any attitude or lifestyle that presupposes or condones hegemony and that does not attend to the voice of the marginalized.

Outline of the Discursive Figurative Structure of 1 Corinthians

1:1-17 Paul, Apostle of Christ Jesus, and the Corinthians, Sanctified in Christ Jesus

A	1:1-9	Called as apostle of Christ and called as partners of Christ
A'	1:10-17	United in the gospel of "the cross of Christ" and its power

1:18–4:21 The Cross as God's Power, Exemplified by the Corinthians and Embodied by Paul

A	1:18-31		The cross, God's wisdom and power
	x	1:18-25	Christ crucified, the power of God, and the wisdom of the world
	x'	1:26-31	The Corinthians chosen by God through Christ crucified
B	2:1–4:7		Paul's Faith in Christ crucified
	x	2:1-16	Paul's endeavor to embody Christ crucified in his ministry
	y	3:1-15	The cross as the foundation of the community

x'	3:16–4:7	The Corinthians' failure to embody Christ crucified
A'	4:8-21	Paul's embodying Christ crucified, a model for the Corinthians

5:1–11:34 The Corinthians' Failure to Embody Christ Crucified; Paul's Exhortation to the Corinthians Calling for Participation in Christ Crucified

A	5:1–6:20	The Corinthians' failure to live Christ crucified
x	5:1-13	Sexual immorality as a case of failure
y	6:1-11	Lawsuit among believers as a case of failure
x'	6:12-20	Solution: "live Christ crucified as members of Christ"
B	7:1–8:13	Paul's advice to the Corinthians who do not embody Christ crucified in their social and community life
x	7:1-40	"Remain with God" in the calling of God as a slave of Christ, not as slaves of human beings
x'	8:1-13	Christ "died" for all in the community; Paul's embodiment of Christ crucified through self-control (not eating meat)
C	9:1-22	Paul's living Christ crucified by becoming weak
B'	9:23–11:1	Paul's exhortation calling for participation in Christ crucified
A'	11:2-34	Community worship and the Lord's Supper through participating in Christ crucified
x	11:2-16	Egalitarian worship service
x'	11:17-34	Proclaiming and participating in Christ crucified

12:1–15:11 Exhortation: The Corinthian Body as *Christic* Embodiment

A	12:1-30	Diversity in the Corinthian body (gifts, services, activities), baptized into one body; the Corinthians as Christic body, Christic embodiment
x	12:1-3	Jesus as Lord
y	12:4-11	Gifts of the Spirit for all (equals)

x'	12:12-30	In order to be the "body of Christ," crucified for "others"
B	12:31–13:13	The Corinthians as loving body
A'	14:1–15:11	The Corinthians called to build a loving community
x	14:1-19	In order to be the "body of Christ," pursue love and build up a community
y	14:20-40	Gifts of the Spirit for all (equals): a hymn, a lesson, a revelation, a tongue, an interpretation
x'	15:1-11	Christ as Lord, died and raised for us

15:12-58 As Christ Crucified Was Raised, So the Crucified Body of Christians Will Be Raised

A	15:12-20	Christ crucified has been raised from the dead
B	15:21-49	The power of the resurrected Christ at work for all the children of Adam (not merely believers), since the crucified and risen Christ is the new Adam
A'	15:50-58	A new kind of body; imperishable (after crucified death) for the "body of Christ"

16:1-24 Conclusion

A	16:1-4	Show your love of the Christ crucified: collection for the saints
A'	16:5-24	Corinthians, stand firm in your faith

Let us examine how the key thematic and figurative features of this structure focus on the figure, "the body of Christ."

1:1-17 Paul, Apostle of Christ Jesus, and the Corinthians, Sanctified in Christ Jesus

This first figurative unit has inverted parallelisms between 1:1-2 and 1:12-17. First Corinthians 1:1-2 presents Paul as an apostle of Christ Jesus and the Corinthians as sanctified in Christ Jesus [*en Christō Iesou*] and saints. But 1:12-17 underscores that being an apostle of Christ (in Paul's case) and sanctified in Christ Jesus (in the Corinthians' case) involve more than membership or belonging. The Corinthians should not say either "I belong to Paul," or "I belong to Apollos," or "I belong to Cephas," or "I belong to Christ" (1:12). This is not what *en Christō Iesou* means; it does not mean "belonging to a party," or to an *ecclesiological body* characterized by a monolithic unity. Similarly, being apostles does not mean baptizing (understood as making members of an ecclesiological body) but bringing and manifesting the good news of "the cross of Christ" which has power and should not be emptied of its power. Thus, being "in Christ" does not mean belonging to an ecclesiological body; the gospel is centered on the cross of Christ as power.

The first sub-unit of 1:1-9 (A) has parallels between "Paul being called as apostle of Christ" (1:1) and the Corinthians being "called into the fellowship of his Son, Jesus Christ our Lord" (1:9). Thus, the *koinōnia* to which the Corinthians are called is like Paul's apostleship, in the sense that the Corinthians have partnership (are partners)[19] with Christ. The second sub-unit of 1:10-17 (A') introduces the cross of Christ, which is the true basis of unity. Being united in the same mind and the same purpose (1:10) is not a matter of belonging to an ecclesiological body, but rather is a matter of having a mind and purpose framed by the same gospel that does not empty the cross of Christ of its power (1:17).

1:18–4:21 The Cross as God's Power Exemplified by the Corinthians and Embodied by Paul

In this second figurative unit, the cross of Christ, introduced in the first figurative unit (1:1-17), is further emphasized. In this unit, inverted parallelisms exist between 1:18-31 and 4:8-21. In 1:18-31 (A) the cross of Christ is shown to be the center of Paul's message as a manifestation of God's power (1:18-25, x)—"the message about the cross is foolishness to those who are perishing, but to us who are being saved it is the power of God" (1:18)—and exemplified by the Corinthians' own cross-like experience at the time of their call (1:26-31, x')—"God chose what is foolish in the world to shame the wise; God chose what is weak in the world to shame the strong; God chose what is low and despised in the world" (1:27-28).

In an inverted way (the second part of a broad chiastic construction), 4:8-21 (A') shows in 4:8-13 Paul's own cross-like experience—"as though sentenced to death . . . fools for the sake of Christ [*dia christon*] . . . weak

... in disrepute ... We have become like the rubbish of the world, the dregs of all things, to this very day" (4:9-13)—as a way of life that the Corinthians have abandoned, in contrast with their original experience. Then the sub-unit concludes (4:14-21), emphasizing that by embodying the cross, by sharing in the crucified "body of Christ," Paul's message also shares in the power of the cross—"For the kingdom of God depends not on talk but on power" (4:20; cf. 1:18)—and thus, the crucified-like Paul has authority as an apostle and father of the Corinthians (4:15), and thus he is in a position to exhort them to "be imitators of me" (4:16). Imitating Paul means precisely sharing with him in the crucified body of Christ (4:8-13).

The sub-unit 2:1–4:7 (B, the body of the figurative unit 1:18–4:21) describes Paul's endeavor to embody Christ crucified in his ministry (2:1-16, x), even as the Corinthians fail to do so. Paul observes their concern to belong to one party or another, to be members of an institutional body (3:16–4:7, x'). Thus Paul is concerned that they conceive of themselves not as "belonging" to one party or another, but they should recognize that "all is yours, and you are of Christ, and Christ is of God" (*humeis de christou, christos de theou*, 3:22-23).

In 2:1-16 (x), Paul affirms that he proclaims (2:2) and embodies (2:3) only Christ crucified, which is the power of God (2:4-5) and the wisdom of God (2:7)—rather than proclaiming the mystery of God with lofty words of wisdom, which is the wisdom of this age (2:2, 11-14). Thus in 3:1-15 (y), Paul speaks of the foundation of the community, "that foundation is Jesus Christ" (3:13); given the figurative organization of these passages, this phrase must be understood as referring to Jesus Christ crucified. It is Christ crucified, as proclaimed, which is the foundation of the community in which "God's fellow workers" are equal (3:9) without dominating each other and without arrogantly claiming "I belong to Paul," or "I belong to Apollos" (3:4). Conversely, those who do not live on the foundation of Christ crucified are people of the flesh, and infants in Christ (3:1-3), as is clear in their behaving according to human inclinations (3:3).

In 3:16–4:7 (x') Paul urges the Corinthians to remember that as a community they are God's temple—"Do you not know [*ouk oidate* plural] that you are [*este* plural] God's temple and that God's Spirit dwells in you [*en humin* plural]?" (3:16). Therefore the only things they can boast of are gifts of God. But as a community they have to live as God's temple in which the Spirit dwells. As the concluding unit (A', 4:8-21) shows, living as God's temple involves imitating Paul's embodiment of Christ crucified (4:8-13).

Thus in 4:15-16 Paul exhorts the Corinthians to imitate "his [my] ways *in Christ Jesus*" (*tas hodos mou tas en christō*, 4:17), that is, to imitate his Christic way of life, being and living in Christ crucified.

5:1–11:34   The Corinthians' Failure to Embody Christ Crucified, Paul's Exhortation to the Corinthians Calling for Participation in Christ Crucified

This figurative unit comprises multiple layers of inverted parallelisms, which addresses the Corinthians' failure to embody Christ crucified in their lives (especially in marriage, community, and social life; 5:1–6:20, A) and exhorts the Corinthians to participate in Christ crucified (11:2-34, A'). The overall inverted parallelism in 5:1–11:34 can be found between 5:1–6:20 (A) and 11:2-34 (A', community worship and the Lord's Supper as participation in Christ crucified).

In 5:1–6:20 (A), as a sub-unit, there is an inverted parallelism between 5:1-13 (x, sexual immorality) and 6:12-20 (x', glorifying God in your body), whereas in the middle section, 6:1-11 (y) presents the role of the Corinthians who must live through sanctification and justification for the Lord Jesus Christ (6:11: "But you were washed, you were sanctified, you were justified in the name of the Lord Jesus Christ and in the Spirit of our God"). The Corinthians failed because they did not live up to the Lord (Christ crucified) and the Spirit. Thus, in 6:12-20 (x'), the solution is to "live Christ crucified" as members of Christ (6:12-20).

Concerning the inverted parallelism between 5:1–6:20 (A) and 11:2-34 (A', community worship and the Lord's Supper as participation in Christ crucified), for our purpose it is enough to note the inverted parallelism between 11:17-34 and 5:1-13.[20] The community becomes a community of Christ crucified when its members truly participate in the Lord's Supper (11:17-34). This true participation in the Lord's Supper means to share Christ crucified in the sense that "our paschal lamb, Christ (crucified), has been sacrificed" (5:7) for us, so that they "celebrate the festival, not with the old yeast, the yeast of malice and evil, but with the unleavened bread of sincerity and truth" (5:8).

The second bracket of inverted parallelisms (B–B') can be found between 7:1–8:13 (Paul's advice to the Corinthians, who do not embody Christ crucified in their social, community life) and 9:23–11:1 (Paul's exhortation for the gospel of participation in Christ crucified) whereas the middle section, 9:1-22 (C), emphasizes Paul's living Christ crucified by becoming weak with the weak.

Within 7:1–8:13 (B) there is also an inverted parallelism between 7:1-40 (x) and 8:1-13 (x'). That is, social life or married life should function with mutual agreement (7:1-16), but its ultimate purpose has to do with not sinning against Christ who died for the weak (8:11-13). Thus, Paul says he would never eat meat if food is a cause of someone's falling (8:13).

Within 9:23–11:1 (B') there is also an inverted parallelism between 9:23-27 and 10:31–11:1. In 9:23-27, Paul's becoming weak enacts the gospel (of Christ), which is explained as "God-centered" (10:31) and "others-centered" (10:32-33) along with his exhortation to "be imitators of me, as I am of Christ" (11:1). Why can he say this? As he expresses in the very center of this unit (C, 9:1-22), Paul's entire ministry is an embodiment of Christ crucified. He lives Christ crucified to make the gospel available to all. Even though Paul is free and has authority as an apostle (9:1), he does not exercise his power and rights because of the gospel of Christ; rather, Paul becomes "a slave to all" (9:19) and is becoming "all things to all" (9:22).

12:1–15:11 Exhortation: The Corinthian Body as *Christic* Embodiment

This figurative unit also has inverted parallelisms between 12:1-30 (A) and 14:1–15:11 (A') and has 12:31–13:13 (B') in the middle. In 12:1-30, the Corinthians as a Christic body—a Christic embodiment has a diversity of gifts, services, and activities. So, such variety in the community should mean that the Corinthians are called to build a loving community, using their gifts of the Spirit for the sake of and with others (14:1–15:11). The middle section 12:31–13:13 (B') then shows a picture of a loving community based on Christ crucified, which is to live for and with others as Christ crucified (12:12-30, Ax'). Within this inverted parallelism, several more inverted ones appear: 12:1-3 (Ax) with 15:1-11 (A'x') clarifying what saying "Jesus is Lord" means, that it refers to Jesus as the Lord who died and who was raised; 12:4-11 (Ay) with 14:20-40 (A'y) clarifying the gifts of the Spirit that are equal, and that all have these gifts for the sake of others; 12:12-30 (Ax') with 14:1-19 (A'x) in terms of the meaning of the "body of Christ" (dying for others and pursuing love).

15:12-58   As Christ Crucified Was Raised, So the Crucified Body of the Christians Will Be Raised

This figurative unit also has an inverted parallelism between 15:12-20 (A) and 15:50-58 (A') with 15:21-49 (B) in the middle. The proclamation that Christ died for us and was raised from the dead (15:12-20) should mean that those who live Christ crucified wear a new body (15:50-58). Then in 15:21-49, the power of the resurrected Christ is at work for all the children of Adam because the crucified and risen Christ is the new Adam.

16:1-24   Conclusion

This last figurative unit concludes the whole letter with its last exhortation to the Corinthians to show "your love" for the saints (16:1-4, A) and to stand firm in "your faith" (16:5-24, A').

Fig. 19. **Representations of the Corinthian body.** *From 44* B.C.E. *on, Corinth presided over the far more ancient Isthmian games, and athletic contests were a source of great civic pride. Under Roman rule, however, athletic prowess also became a metaphor for military might, and victory, whether military or athletic, was ascribed to the favor of Fortune (*Fortuna; *Greek* Tychē). *Here a mosaic, laid in the time of Augustus or Tiberius, depicts a nude athlete after his triumph, presenting himself before the goddess Good Luck (*Eutychia).

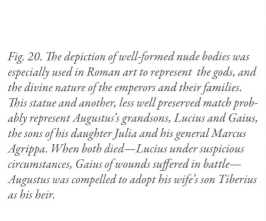

Fig. 20. The depiction of well-formed nude bodies was especially used in Roman art to represent the gods, and the divine nature of the emperors and their families. This statue and another, less well preserved match probably represent Augustus's grandsons, Lucius and Gaius, the sons of his daughter Julia and his general Marcus Agrippa. When both died—Lucius under suspicious circumstances, Gaius of wounds suffered in battle—Augustus was compelled to adopt his wife's son Tiberius as his heir.

Figs. 21 and 22. These terra-cotta representations of body parts were discovered buried in caches in the sacred precinct of Asklepius, god of healing. Manufactured in the fourth century B.C.E., they were available for use as votive offerings for persons who came to the god's shrine in search of healing. As mementos of illness or injury healed, they bear a striking contrast to the imagery of bodily wholeness that prevailed in Roman Corinth.

Figs. 23 and 24. At shared ritual meals, Corinthians would recline on cushioned benches, invoke the gods, and enjoy conversation and entertainment. The benches in these dining rooms show the intimate settings in which such sacred meals took place.

——— The Life of the Christic Body in Corinth ———

Given the figurative structure of 1 Corinthians outlined previously, the letter can be subdivided into three thematic parts, respectively focused on the themes of the cross (1:18–4:21; 5:1–11:34), the community (12:1–15:11), and transformation (15:12-58).[21] These three key theological themes all involve a figural representation of the body of Christ. Further, the three themes are mutually implicated in the discursive structure of the letter as they are related to faith, love, and hope. The following table suggests the complex role of these three "body figures" in the letter. (The table does not indicate either chronology or causal relations from left to right; rather, it seeks to suggest the interrelationship of the three main "body figures": Christ crucified as body figure, the community as body figure, and the resurrection as body figure.)

Table 2. Body Figures

	The Cross (1:18–4:21; 5:1–11:34)	The Community (12:1–15:11)	Transformation (15:12-58)
Image of body figure	Christ crucified as foundation of faith, of Paul's apostleship, of the Corinthians as saints (1:18–4:21), and of the community (5:1–11:34)	The Corinthian *body* as Christic embodiment	Resurrection *body* as living through Christ crucified
Theology of body figure	Faith	Love	Hope

The Cross (1:18–4:21; 5:1–11:34)

In 1:18–4:21, the image of the crucified body of Christ (1:23; 2:2) plays a central role, primarily doing two things: it provides a symbolic identification with the liminal experience of the marginalized (slaves in particular), and it deconstructs human power, wisdom, charismatic gifts, self-seeking glory, or dominating unity.[22]

Regarding the symbolic identification with the liminal experience of the marginalized—if Paul's audience comes primarily from the lower class as indicated in 1:26 ("not many of you were wise by human standards, not many were powerful, not many were of noble birth"), they seem to associate their suffering and marginal experience with the crucified Christ. The idea of the cross is foolish to the Greeks but concretely manifests God's power to those who suffer in the world (1:18). For them, therefore, the crucified Christ is a window through which they see the world differently, finding a redemptive message in God who values all life. Paul declares: "But God chose what is foolish in the world to shame the wise; God chose what is weak in the world to shame the strong; God chose what is low and despised in the world, things that are not, to reduce to nothing things that are, so that no one might boast in the presence of God" (1:27-28).

Here the message for the lower-class people struggling to live a cross-like life is twofold. On the one hand, God will reverse the course of history to affirm the life of the weak, and even the cross cannot stop God's power of resurrection. On the other hand, the cross is not a necessary and sufficient condition for resurrection; nor is it warranted to bring resurrection. The cross is an unwanted, unnecessary evil. So the message of the cross here is not to affirm the cross experience as such, but to resist it because the cross-like life is destructive. In sum, for those who suffer, part of the message of the cross is God's solidarity with the suffering Christ. Those who suffer are comforted and encouraged to stand up with God's promise of victory.[23]

In this realistic, twofold sense of the cross (solidarity and unwanted suffering), the theology of Christ's so-called vicarious death is hardly to be recognized, because in such a case the suffering are not helped at all; they continue to suffer. Indeed, the theme of Jesus' vicarious death can implicitly perpetuate or condone injustice by discouraging resistance to the evil of the cross.

The message of the cross of Christ also addresses the powerful with the challenge to deconstruct human power and wisdom. To that end, Paul establishes a series of oppositions:

Christ crucified as foolishness	versus	Christ crucified as God's power (1:18);
the wisdom of the wise, the wisdom of the world	versus	the wisdom of God (1:19-21);
knowing God through wisdom	versus	knowing God through the foolishness of the proclamation of the cross (1:21);
Christ crucified as a stumbling block and foolishness	versus	Christ crucified as God's power and God's wisdom (1:23-4);
God's foolishness	versus	human wisdom;
God's weakness	versus	human strength (1:25);
proclaiming the mystery of God in lofty words	versus	proclaiming Christ crucified (2:2);
"we" who live as fools for the sake of Christ	versus	"you" who are wise in Christ (4:10);
we who are weak	versus	you who are strong;
we who are held in disrepute	versus	you who are held in honor (4:10).

Through all these oppositions, the image of Christ crucified (the crucified body) deconstructs human powers, because for Paul the human problem has to do with a "denial of death," denial of sacrifice, and the pursuit of a life in glory at the expense of others. So here the message of "dying and living" calls for a voluntary cost of love for all. In this sense, the cross is the voluntary price and sacrifice for others in the beloved community.

The crucified body, as a figure of comfort for the downtrodden in the community and as a figure of God's power, becomes the basis of the Corinthian community, one which should live out the gospel of dying love while remembering the historical past of Jesus' faithfulness. As seen in the previously described figurative structure of 1 Corinthians 1–4, a spirit-ruled embodiment of Christ (2:6-16) is the key to the community. In other words, for Paul, the spirit-ruled person is a body ruled by the Spirit of God, and at the same time, a crucified body, as is the case with Paul himself (2:1-5). In 1 Corinthians 3, Paul foregrounds the Corinthians who boast of human wisdom and power: "for you are still of the flesh. For as long as there is jealousy and quarreling among you, are you not of the flesh, and behaving according to human inclinations?" (3:3). Paul further asks: "Do you not know that you are God's temple and that God's Spirit dwells in you?" (3:16). Lastly, asking the audience to imitate him (4:1), Paul sternly challenges them to return to a "crucified living" just as Paul himself embodies in his life (4:1-21). Paul asks the Corinthians to imitate him because he lives in Christ crucified (4:16-17). Paul thoroughly expresses his theology or ethics in Christ crucified (4:9-13): ". . . as though sentenced to death, . . . a spectacle to the world, . . . fools for the sake of Christ, . . . hungry and thirsty, . . . poorly clothed and beaten and homeless, . . . weary, . . . reviled, . . . persecuted, . . . like the rubbish of the world, the dregs of all things, to this very day."

In 5:1–11:34, responding to all the failures to embody Christ crucified that he observes in the community (sexual immorality, lawsuits, marriage life, food offered to idols, and the Lord's Supper), Paul proposes as a solution that the Corinthian community and their social life be cross-like. As shown in the figurative structure, the Corinthians (6:1-11) should live through sanctification and justification because of the Lord Jesus Christ. In continuation, in 6:12-20, the solution is posed clearly in terms of living Christ crucified as "members of Christ" because some Corinthians did not live up to the Spirit, who requires sanctification and justification. In

6:15, Paul's answer to a rhetorical question—"Do you not know that your bodies are members of Christ? Should I therefore take the members of Christ and make them members of a prostitute? Never!"—shows that the term *members* does not connote members of the community in the sense of an organism. Rather, from the perspective of the figurative structure of the text, and the centrality of the figure of Christ crucified, it means to live like Christ, in solidarity with Christ, who showed his faithfulness through a suffering death (Christ crucified). The climactic point in terms of Paul's exhortation to live with Christ crucified appears at the end of this unit 5:1–11:34, namely, in 11:17-34, in which true transformation can happen through participating in the death of Christ, embracing all people regardless of gender, class, or any other distinction.

To further support the claim that the cross is offered as a figure of the life Paul proposes as a solution, we may observe that in the middle of this unit Paul explains why bearing the cross is necessary (9:23–11:1), and how he himself experiences the death of Christ in his life and ministry (9:1-22). The reason for taking the cross is the gospel, which is God-centered and others-centered ("So, whether you eat or drink, or whatever you do, do everything for the glory of God. Give no offense to Jews or to Greeks or to the church of God" 10:31-32). For the sake of this gospel of Christ, Paul becomes Christ-like and "all things to all people" (9:19-22). Thereby, Paul urges the Corinthians to "be imitators of me, as I am of Christ" (11:1). Similarly, earlier in 4:16 Paul exhorts them to "be imitators of me" right after his mention of his Christ-like, cross-like experience (4:10-15). Paul clarifies that he preaches only Christ crucified (2:2) and that he does it even through death-like, foolish experience (4:10-16). In both instances, Paul clearly reveals to the Corinthians why they should imitate him, because he embodies in his life the death of Christ. In this perspective, "being imitators of me, as I am of Christ" (11:1) has nothing to do with membership in a community, but everything to do with being Christ-like. Paul talks about his status as "being all things to all people," just as Christ was.

The Community as Christic Embodiment (12:1–15:11)

The Corinthian body as "body of Christ" (12:26) connotes two things: a metaphor for living like Christ and a community or *ekklēsia* representing Christ in their bodies. It is important to distinguish between Paul's use of "body of Christ" as Christic embodiment and "ekklēsia" (1 Cor 14:4) as an assembly or an institution. In the *ekklēsia*, all kinds of people, differentiated in terms of gender, class, and ethnicity, should live up to the spirit of Christ, especially in Christ crucified, which deconstructs the Corinthian cases of disembodiment and reconstructs the community of diversity for all (12-14). In the figurative system of 1 Corinthians, this figure of the body (12:12-26) should not be read as an organism metaphor but as a figure promoting the embodiment of Christ culminating in v. 27: "*now* you are *body of Christ* and individually *limbs* of it"). "You" should embody Christ in your bodies through dying with Christ. The parsing of v. 27 (present, indicative, second person, and plural) emphasizes the Corinthian embodiment of the Christic body: "you" (plural) are agents to live out "body of Christ" (*sōma christou*). These agents should work hard to include more people in the love of Christ and to live out the gospel of Christ in their bodies. It is an urgent business of "now" (*de*) in verse 27 that shifts the mood dramatically from body analogy (12:12-26) to an exhortation for the community (12:27). Now the Corinthian community should live the "body of Christ" in their social, community life. For Paul, bodily life is relational, involving all aspects of human life, as Janssen writes:[24]

> Paul employs "body," "members," "weapons," and "you yourselves," as parallel expressions: they do not designate separate parts of the human organism, but existence as a whole. To exist means bodiliness, being defined and conditioned, a lack of freedom, being integrated into structural context of injustice and sin. To be soma means, therefore, that nothing in life is neutral. We are relational beings, related to one another. "In Christ," however, we become capable of righteousness: this is what Paul affirms in Rom 6:12-14.

With this kind of holistic bodily life, Paul envisions a community of Christic embodiment, which requires believers (members of the community) to place their members, their capabilities, their potential, their active commitment at the service of ongoing community life.[25] The Corinthian community as an agent of Christic embodiment cannot stop their work or wait idly for a mere future consummation. Rather, it is to be an *ekklēsia* of loving community, a theme to which I turn next (12:31–13:13).

A Loving Body (12:31–13:13)

A loving community cannot stand still but moves on and strives for an eschatological fulfillment of now in the sense that the community lives now the end time—the vision of a loving community through faith, hope, and love. We may conceive this community using an analogy of a tricycle cart, having each wheel represented by faith, hope, and love. In this image, the order in the relationship between faith, hope, and love is unimportant; each wheel is equally important. This tricycle can move along with faith, hope, and love; if one wheel is missing, it is incomplete and cannot move forward. From a community perspective,[26] faith, hope, and love are interrelated and should work together for the common goal, which is to move the community forward, making it alive for all people under any circumstances.[27] Similarly, we can relate this tricycle cart image to Christ's faithfulness and love, which continue toward an eschatological hope.[28]

Such a loving community is an urgent matter for the community because the community was so divided, boasting of its spiritual gifts as we see in 1 Corinthians 14. The urgent need is to re-emphasize the centrality of love for community rebuilding. Paul's appeal to love is the most effective way to respond to the situation of division. What is at stake for the Corinthian community is to become a loving and caring community without fighting for spiritual hegemony. To build community, Paul emphasizes the importance of love in the context of the holistic life together. Individually, neither faith alone, nor hope, nor love can sustain community; rather, as with the tricycle image, the community must become at once loving, faithful, and hopeful (1 Cor 12:31–13:13). In sum, the primary teachings of 12:31–13:13 are the community's love, vision, and action.

In 12:31–13:3, love should be understood in terms of Christ crucified (1:23; 2:2) in whom one can find Christ's concrete expression of love for the poor and the downtrodden (1:27). Love is more than lofty words or human wisdom or knowledge. It is deep empathy associated with the rock-bottom experiences of the poor and the social outcasts. This love is not a solitary, once-and-for-all event achieved by Christ. Even all-powerful faith, or speaking in tongues, or understanding all knowledge and mysteries is, in the end, meaningless without love in the community (13:1-2) in which all members are important and respected (12:12-26). Without love, "I am nothing" and "I gain nothing" (13:2-3). Faith without love is nothing! Faith without love is incomplete.

In 13:4-7, such a love is not an individual or psychological thing. Rather, it denotes relational, others-oriented, community love whose characteristics include being "patient, kind, and not being arrogant or rude" (13:4).

"Love does not seek its own" (13:5) shows a community perspective and vision; it lays out a clear responsibility for all of the members in the community. Such community love does not rejoice at wrong, but rejoices in the right (13:6). Furthermore, such community-oriented love is expressed with action verbs (13:4-7; all love-words are verbs, not adjectives or nouns).[29] Love works for others, and it is not self-centered. This love bears all things, believes all things, hopes all things, and endures all things (13:7). In other words, this love, along with faith and hope, must go through "all things" that involve an ongoing struggle of the Corinthian community.

In 13:8-13, such love never ends (13:8) as the community moves on until the end. Prophecies pass away, tongues cease, and knowledge also passes away. Whereas love is complete, knowledge and prophecy are incomplete (13:9). Love is complete in the sense that it binds the community so that the community can continue to strive for an eschatological fulfillment. But knowledge and prophecy can be childish ways that cause members of the community to fight for hegemony without striving for the community of love (13:11). Therefore, faith, hope, and love abide (13:13a) in a holistic community. Through them, the eschatological community makes sense without losing the power of love in the present. In other words, this verse gives us a complete picture of the fluidity of the community constantly on the move.

Taking the Measure of Love (1 Corinthians 13)

I have attempted to read the *love* chapter (1 Corinthians 13) from the perspective of a holistic, Christic community. This reading differs from other prominent readings; I contend that it best fits Paul's ethics in the context of power conflicts where an individualistic, disembodied faith demonizes "others."

Reading 1: Love as a Divine Gift—forensic, individualistic model[30]

On one reading of love in 1 Corinthians, the hermeneutical frame is structured by a forensic understanding of God's salvation according to which believers are declared righteous by faith, "once and for all," through Christ's vicarious death. In this reading, love, *agape,* is godly in origin, God's unconditional love for human beings. The divine source of love[31] is expressed in the translation of love in 13:4: "love is patient; love is kind" (all these describing the godly character of love); literally "love suffers long; love acts kindly; it does not envy or boast or puff up itself."[32] In this view, chapter 13 is sometimes considered as a hymn inserted into the letter, not Paul's own work.[33]

Love, *agape*, is also what should characterize the life of those who benefited from God's love, not because they have the ability to love but because it is given to them in their personal relationship with God. It is another and the most important gift of the Spirit (12:31).

Reading 1 meets the needs of people who are concerned about personal security or identity. However, this interpretation of God's love in a forensic and individualistic context does not contribute to envisioning a holistic community for all. Moreover, this kind of forensic understanding of individual salvation can contribute to excluding others with a narrow vision of the community; what is essential here is simply the individual's faith in Christ. Whereas this reading hinges on an individualistic view of love, preoccupied with a personal relationship with God, my reading is a community-centered view of love, and so emphasizes the *human* part of love as necessary and good. From this perspective, where the community is the central concern, this love cannot concern only personal relationships. But this love should be a vision of the community with which members are capable of loving. In that regard, God's love or salvation is not an object that we can possess "once and for all," but it is actualized every day, moving forward to God's loving community for all.

Reading 2: Love as a Command[34]

Reading 2 complements Reading 1 in that it emphasizes an ethical responsibility based on a forensic understanding of love. God's gracious love for us calls for specific responses, such as thanksgiving and obedience to God. Thus, in Reading 2, the action of love (13:4-7) is a legitimate response to the once-and-for-all love of God. The human problem here is a lack of will or obedience to God. Reading 2 is an indicative-imperative model, one I have called a two-step ethics in the sense that one acts based on duty or indebtedness (so "become what you are"), whereas my reading provides a one-step ethics in the sense that there is no division between identity and practice.[35] Certainly, Reading 2 is helpful for those who lack an ethical sense of who they are and motivates them to participate in

God's ongoing work. Whereas Reading 1 does not emphasize the ethical part of loving as a second step, Reading 2 spells out the ethical responsibility although responsibility is limited to an individual level.

Reading 3: Love as a Radical Challenge—liberation, feminist model[36]

In a third reading, love has to do with self-affirmation and empowerment of the oppressed and the marginalized.[37] In this reading, selflessness or self-sacrifice is not viewed positively because the oppressors will exacerbate the abusive situations of the oppressed. Likewise, liberation theologians draw our attention to the social dimension of Christian love, as Gustavo Gutierrez explains:[38]

> The tendency to consider Christian love only in terms of one-to-one relationships has been criticized by theologians of political, liberationist, and ecological orientations alike. Love must not be reduced to a private sentiment, nor to a mere object of belief. Love must inspire and guide Christian faith, hope and action for the coming of God's kingdom.

In this way, 1 Corinthians 13 is read through the eyes of the marginalized and understood as a transformative message of radical love (13:1-3). Love does not rejoice at wrong but rejoices in the right. Such a radical love demands to bear all things, believe all things, hope all things, and endure all things. Reading 3 is close to the reading I have outlined previously in terms of a radical challenge to the hegemonic voice of society, but my reading involves a broader-based conception of a community beyond identity politics and that includes all.

Reading 4: Love as Interpersonal Faith[39]

In Reading 4, love is acted out through interpersonal faith, which is very different from the forensic interpretation. Faith here means an imitation of Christ crucified and does not absolutize anything; it is *interpersonal* in character because it engages *others* who become a type of Christ. Likewise, Paul's typology focuses on a type, a promise, a fulfillment of Jesus that continues to live through believers.[40] Here people must be freed from bondage to the "rulers of this age" and other idolatrous "powers" (1 Cor 2:8; 15:24). Faith envisions interpersonal manifestations of God's power and love in the world. The interpersonal aspect of faith changes our attitude toward others. What is at stake in the community is to accept others as they are. In this perspective of reading, the action of love (13:4-7) is a manifestation of faith; it recognizes others in whom we see Christ-like manifestations, also seeing them as better than ourselves not because they are like us (in the community) but because they are unlike us.

Reading 4 is close to my conception of the community where mutual respect and humility is the key to a healthy community that involves all in their diversity.[41] In Reading 4, Jesus, as a type of God's faithfulness, does not resolve all human problems "once and for all." Thus Christ-like manifestations of love should occur to Paul, other leaders of the church, all the members of the community who are *not like us*, and outsiders who are *not like us*. We should see others as better than we are, and love them as persons to whom we are indebted. Thus, Christ invites us to join him in a journey of faith, hope, and love in the community where people are inter-related and interdependent for their existence. The existence of "others" is not something to remove or simply overcome but to live through because we may learn from them Christ-like manifestations. In an individualis-tic faith and life context today, what is at stake is how to reconstruct a community for "all"—in which the rich and the poor, the happy and the unhappy, gather together in acknowledging others, comforting and being comforted, challenging and being challenged. In this regard, my commu-nity-centered reading helps us to envision such an open community for all—affirming "others" (13:1-3) as others, yet not losing the vision of *common humanity in difference*.

The Call to Build a Loving Community (14:1–15:11)

In 14:1–15:11, we see Paul's specific exhortations that the community live and love in the spirit of mutual acceptance and affirmation. Paul is concerned about hegemonic attitudes on the part of those speaking in tongues who disregard those who do not (14:2, 6-12). In light of this spe-cific power conflict in the community, his exhortation begins with the command "pursue (or seek after) love" (*diōkete tēn agapēn*, 14:1), actualiz-ing the discourse on love in the preceding chapter. Again, we see here that

Paul's rhetoric does not imply that the community lacks order (hierarchy), "unity," or specific spiritual gifts. Rather, what is essential is how those spiritual gifts are employed in the context of a loving *ekklēsia* (not, that is, for individualistic purposes) and through a Christic embodiment of faith, love, and hope. There follow in 14:6-32 Paul's instructions regarding specific cases, instructions to encourage one another, and to exercise one's own gifts in building up the *ekklēsia*.

Paul is also concerned to nourish a community in which all members, both male and female, participate as equals. Here in chapter 14, the issue is not who does or does not speak in tongues (the implication is that all in the community can receive free spiritual gifts of God), but how the ethos or benefits of the community may be maintained without disruption. In light of Paul's concern for a ministry of equals in the community, the silencing of women in 14:34-35 hardly fits. That is why many scholars think that these verses are an interpolation made by later copyists or editors. The idea of interpolation has merit, as we observe the very similar wording in one of non-Pauline Pastoral epistles, 1 Tim 2:11-15. But I regard these verses as authentic because (as Antoinette Clark Wire has argued) the external evidence for interpolation is inconclusive at best. On the other hand, while Wire and Elisabeth Schüssler Fiorenza read these verses as Paul's own voice, showing him to be a social conservative who in fact harshly silences women's voices,[42] I argue to the contrary that these verses reflect *not* Paul's own voice, but those of male hierarchical leaders in Corinth. Given the fact that women freely participate in worship and prophesy (1 Corinthians 11) in a community where charismatic gifts are equally available for all (chap. 14), it seems hardly likely that 14:34-35 give voice to Paul's own effort to silence women. Though I agree with Wire and Schüssler Fiorenza that the Corinthian women prophets *were* being suppressed by male hierarchical leaders, I disagree with their identification of that hierarchical position with Paul himself. Instead, I contend, following David Odell-Scott, that these verses represent Paul's *critique* of the hegemonic patriarchal voice *in the community*. As Odell-Scott argues, these lines

> were a direct quotation from a letter from Corinth or from reports of positions taken up in Corinth which were delivered to Paul, and which he quoted in order to make clear precisely the position to which his reply was a direct, straightforward critique in v. 36.[43]

In this view, the direct address in verse 36 is not to women prophets, as suggested by Wire, but is Paul's stinging rebuke to those who would exercise masculine power over women: "What! Did the word of God begin with *you*? Or are *you* the only ones to have received it?"

The Christic Body and the Raised Body of Christ (15:12-58)

The confession of hope in the resurrection body (or "spiritual body") is a major theme in chapter 15. Addressing a struggling, conflicted community, Paul advises them to trust in God with patience (15:35-49).

If we read Paul as a "practical" theologian, responding to present conflicts caused by ideologies both inside and outside of the community, we may conclude that *the present situation of the community* is in his view even as he talks about the past resurrection of Christ and the future resurrection of believers. Note his use of the present tense to describe how resurrection "works," using an organic metaphor of regular, seasonal transformation: a seed is sown, God "gives" a body, what is sown is raised (15:42-44). The contrast between the physical body and the spiritual body is expressed in the present tense as well:

What is sown is perishable	What is raised is imperishable
Dishonor	Glory
Weakness	Power
Physical body (what is sown)	Spiritual body (what is raised)

The appeal, in the present tense, to natural, organic metaphors implies that a regular sequence is expected: death yields to life. Paul speaks again and again of the appropriateness or even necessity of dying: of Christ's death "for our sins" (15:3), of his own "daily" dying (15:31), of those who have already died, and of the "dying" of a seed in the ground (15:35-36). But if dying is as necessary to living again in the Spirit, just like a change in seasons, then the implicit "logic" of the moral life is that dying to one way of life will give way to a new way of life.

In light of the letter's broader exhortation regarding the life of the Christic body, this implicit sequence—death leads to life—suggests that participation in the Christic body *now* should be a matter of practicing one kind of dying. Note that in the series of parallelisms in 15:42-44, each second term results from the first term. Applied to a situation of power conflicts in the Corinthian community, we may infer that (in Paul's view) those who think they have "immortal" bodies, and who seek to exert power over others not wishing to die, should in effect practice a kind of dying: "what you sow does not come to life unless it dies" (15:35). In contrast, those who affirm the resurrection of the dead through a "living out" of dying—that is, through self-emptying and other-affirming life—are putting on immortal and imperishable bodies. Even here, then, the body imagery[44] of death and resurrection suggests a message of protest against hegemonic attitudes and a call for the manifestation of God in the *social* body, the community.[45]

If we relate this discussion to the Corinthian community's disembodiment of the Christic body, we may regard what Paul says about the resurrection as implicitly referring to a transformation of the *Christic* body, in the socio-political and economic reality of people living at the margins of the empire.[46] In other words, participation in the Christic body (*sōma*) must be understood holistically as participation in specific practices, in a world where real bodies are humiliated, tortured, and sickened by various powers, both social and physical.[47] Christ so suffered in his own body; how could the participation in the Christic body be different?

The reality of a world in which human bodies are attacked and destroyed is the necessary context for a full understanding of Paul's rhetoric regarding the resurrection of the dead. The apostle's interest is not merely in theoretical questions regarding the future status of resurrection or the question "what kind of body" enjoys resurrection (15:35), as many readers have understood this chapter.[48] Rather, as we know from his writings (see 2 Corinthians 4), Paul was aware of the abundance of broken bodies, ravaged women, and the suffering of children; he knew in his own body the experiences of living on the margins, feeling hunger, being afflicted, beaten, and scourged. How could his language of the dying and rising body not have immediate contact with his own participation in the Christic body, a liminal experience at the boundaries of society?

It is in this very real life setting that Paul speaks of "the splendor of God's power, which will transform all things" and which says "yes" to devalued bodies exploited by war, terror, slavery, and inhumaneness.[49] We simply cannot deny the context of Paul's own life as a participation in the world of broken bodies, here and there under the Roman Empire and in particular at Corinth. As Claudia Janssen says, Paul "has these ravaged bodies before his mind's eye, and when he speaks of splendor (*doxa*, Rom 8:18), he sees the bodies of children who starve and women who are raped. He assures them that they are valuable, that they bear the resurrection in themselves, and that they are temples of the Holy Spirit (1 Cor 3:16; 6:19)."[50]

Reading the resurrection body as a metaphor allows us to recognize Paul's use of "spiritual body" as part of a rhetorical strategy. Paul argues against a hegemonic, dominating ideology that legitimizes the destruction of human bodies; instead, he affirms God's power, God's "yes" to the body and to life (15:24-25). The rhetoric of the "spiritual body" is a counter-argument against an ideology of the "physical body" alone, an ideology that seeks "fleshly" (that is, manipulative) power, that seeks to evade death but depends upon the sacrifices of other lives. The seed of that ideology must die, Paul warns, to bring forth a new life—the life of the spiritual body, the realm of God enlivened by God's power and God's Spirit. This is a message of God's power, God's mystery, God's "yes" to the world where the downtrodden and the hopeless live.

Paul's point is not to assert a dualism between the body (or flesh) and the spirit; neither does his message of the spiritual body "promote a better life after death; rather, it shows how resurrection can transform the present life."[51] The time of resurrection is not a separated future moment, but is any time now as the future impinges upon the present, "in an instant, in the twinkling of an eye" (15:52). The future engages the world with the challenge to live out the life of the spiritual body, here and now.[52]

Resurrection involves a somatic existence—a participation in the Christic *sōma*—in the everyday setting of Corinth.[53] Resurrection occurs in the community as it includes all aspects of bodily life and allows for God's mystery and power to come into the somatic struggle for justice. Such a commitment to live according to the Spirit is to live as a spiritual body through God's power. Understanding the "body of Christ" as a metaphor for "living out Christ," I suggest that Paul calls the Corinthians to live out the Christic body in order to reconstruct the loving *ekklēsia* not by imposing a notion of unity but by following Christ holistically, accepting diversity.

Reimagining the "body of Christ" as Christ crucified is a key to understanding what Christ's body has to do with our world today. The message of Christ crucified speaks of the power of solidarity, in the same way that

God is with those who are weak and vulnerable (1 Cor 1:17-31). This message brings empowerment and comfort to all broken bodies in all forms, physical or social, even as they live on the margins. On the other hand, Christ crucified is also a symbol that God will turn the world upside down, just as God raised Christ crucified. The word of the cross plays a deconstructing role over against the ideology of those who seek power at the expense of others. Christ crucified becomes a symbol of God's justice, reminding the strong of what Christ sacrificed his life for. This metaphor of Christ crucified challenges us to see the world in a new way, through participation in Christic embodiment.

Practicing the Diversity of Christ's Body

Having come full circle, I return now to the question raised in the Introduction: Is there another way of reading the "body of Christ" and the world today? The answer is a resounding yes; it is a reading from the perspective of a world of diversity, a reading on the part of diversity and for the sake of diversity. Diversity resides in God's very creation; diversity is God's intent, and the world lives by it. Throughout this book, I have shown that Christ's body can be regarded best through the lens of diversity because the problems of the Corinthians lie in a failure to honor the diversity of others. The metaphor of Christ's body plays the role of both deconstructing and reconstructing the Corinthian community so that it might live again with the spirit of diversity. In this chapter, I wish to pursue the questions: Why is diversity necessary in biblical interpretation? What does diversity look like, and how can we honor diversity in interpretation?

Recently, biblical scholars and theologians alike have come to recognize the affirmation of diversity in the biblical text. Theodore Hiebert, for example, finds the motif of diversity when he reads the story of the Tower of Babel (Gen 9). That is, as Cynthia Campbell states, "the problem from God's point of view is that people have not *scattered*, but rather have chosen to stay together."[1] The problem from God's point of view is not human pride or arrogance—as if people were invading the realm of heaven by building a high tower, but their not *scattering*. They had *one* language, which hints at an enforced unity and conformity of an imperial city.[2] But God scatters them by *mixing* (Hebrew *balal*) language so that the people of the Tower of Babel might live in diversity, speaking different languages, moving away from a monocultural system of imperial control.[3] Using the motif of diversity found in Genesis 9, Campbell especially connects it to God's creation story and to the story of Noah in which God blesses the human family: "be fruitful and multiply, fill the earth" (Gen 1:28; 9:1, 8). Campbell's theological conclusion seems right, that diversity would be *God's providential care of the world.*[4] Diversity is a moving force that maintains God's created world as is.

To be sure, the Bible also speaks with a certain hostility to diversity. If we deny or exclude others in our conception of the community, others are expelled from our common space—something we see in the conquest narrative in the book of Joshua that legitimates Israel's story at the expense of "others." No Canaanite story has been recorded.[5] Similarly, in Nehemiah and Ezra, we find a dominant, hegemonic voice of nationalism (or traditionalism) which does not allow "otherness"—followed by the terrible consequence of Israel expelling all foreign spouses. In contrast to these texts, however, the books of Ruth and Jonah challenge such a narrow conception of unity. It is surprising to see in the book of Jonah such a radical message of God's love extending to the people of Nineveh—a love that Jonah, the Israelite, finds hard to imagine, a love even for Israel's enemies. Ruth and Jonah witness the episodes of God's love; it is a love that has no limit, as the sun shines on all. We learn from these witnesses that the notion of the community is incomplete, as long as *others* are left out in God's world.

Jesus seems to point similarly to the importance of community in his encounter with a young ruler who asked, "What shall I do to inherit eternal life?" (Luke 18:18-23). This ruler says that he kept all the commandments since his youth. Then Jesus answers: "There is still one thing lacking. Sell all that you own and distribute the money to the poor, and you will have treasure in heaven; then come, follow me" (Luke 18:22). In light of a broader conception of the community, a young ruler's eternal life would be incomplete or meaningless because eternal life should share life with the poor (others). The implications of this episode go beyond personal ethics; the meaning of eternal life relates unavoidably to the existence of others. As long as there are others who are not part of the community, the community is undone. We see, then, that some biblical texts point to the existence of "others" as a hermeneutical lens through which we might better see things otherwise not easily seen or heard.

Diversity is necessary because our life, as a God-given diverse life, takes diverse forms of thought, experience, culture, and social life. Diversity arises from *differences or complexities* in our life, as well as in the text, as we live in different parts of the world, speaking different languages, and cherishing different values and cultures. The existence of diversity and complexity in our lives requires the recognition of diversity in our approaches, because one method or one approach cannot comprehend the complexities of life and the multiple dimensions of the written text.[6] Because of such complexities and differences, we should leave room for "heteronomy" (rule by others)—for an intervening space of God's mystery by which "others" come into our discourse.[7]

Diversity as Discernment

Because of complexities or differences in our life (and the text), we need an ongoing dialogue with *others*,[8] which means that diversity is not simply fixed or a given. Diversity means more than mere differences of culture or people. Phenomenal differences themselves, whatever they are, do not automatically constitute diversity. Such differences, whether positive or negative, must come into a critical dialogue with each other, with openness and a humbling spirit.[9] For instance, in the case of the Corinthian issue of food offered to idols, some know that they can eat it without a problem; others do not eat it because of their conscience. This difference between the strong and the weak can be resolved through mutual dialogue and mutual understanding, which is not based on "either/or" thinking but on a holistic view of community—a relational, edifying community. In other words, there should not be absolute norms regarding food offered to idols. That is, some people may or may not eat in a certain situation. Through engagement with one another, relational, communal love overwrites the abstract, dominant knowledge of some who do not care about the existence of others. Because of this, Paul declares: "if food is a cause of their falling, I will never eat meat" (1 Cor 8:13). He continues: "Food will not bring us close to God. We are no worse off if we do not eat, and no better off if we do" (1 Cor 8:8). In this sense, diversity does not simply allow all differences, as they are, as if they had ontological value or presence. By distinguishing between diversity and differences in this way, we can develop and maintain a sense of balance between being critical and self-critical while celebrating differences and diversity.

Diversity as Balance

Complexity or differences in our life (and the text) do not allow for nihilism or relativism because interpreters must assume ethical responsibility for their reading. Therefore, there should be a sense of balance in diversity, for example, between the individual liberty of speaking in tongues (agency) and communal responsibility. In other words, diversity should be understood in the way that respect is given to those who do not understand those speaking in tongues. On the other hand, diversity also should be understood in the way that that same respect is given to those speaking in tongues, insofar as there is discernment in the community. That is, individual (personal) agency should not be stopped except for the purpose of edifying the community. Throughout the letter of First Corinthians, we read for this sort of balance to be struck between personal agency and responsibility for the community. Although Paul instructs the community to care for the *ekklēsia* as a whole, there are also empowered individuals who are prophesying, praying, and speaking in tongues—women being part of that powerhouse.

——————— Christ's Body and Multiculturalism ———————

In his article "Neither Jew nor Greek: Multiculturalism and the New Perspective on Paul," John M.G. Barclay suggests that Paul's radical vision of God's grace for all leads to multiculturalism, as he states:[10]

> The foundation of Paul's gospel, and the basis of his relativization of all cultures, is his radical appreciation of the grace of God which humbles human pride and subverts the theological and cultural edifices which "flesh" constructs. . . . The church exists not for its own sake but to bear witness to the grace of God. Paul himself is ultimately speechless before the mercy of God and cannot find even Christian language in which to express its significance (Rom 11:33-36). To this extent, even Pauline theology could be mobilized to serve a multiculturalism whose religious basis is the affirming and relativizing grace of God.

In the same vein, my rendering of Paul's central theology and ethics leads to multiculturalism because, as I showed through this book, the gospel of the crucified Christ (1 Cor 1:23; 2:2; Gal 6:14; see also Phil 3:18; Gal 3:1) embraces all people in different cultures. With or through the work of Christ crucified, God's love (grace) continues to flow to all people who need a new life of love and respect, for which Christ lived and died.

Seen this way, the gospel of the crucified Christ has at least two implications for multiculturalism and/or interreligious dialogue. The first one relates to the message of encouragement and comfort for those who suffer like Christ. The cross is God's solidarity for them. The other relates to the message of God's harsh critique for those who overpower others; here the cross deconstructs the self-seeking glory of the powerful. If we take this double-edged gospel of the crucified Christ, we can focus on the work of God's justice in today's world. Toward this end, as Bassler notes, believers are supposed to live like Christ, proclaiming Christ's death in which they participate and sharing his radical vision of God's love for all people.[11] Likewise, Christ's suffering is not finished but continues. If we reimagine Christ's body as the crucified body of Christ, which is at the center of Paul's theology and ethics, the implication of Christ's body goes well beyond metaphorical organism in which unity is so emphasized, often at the expense of diversity. If we focus on the work of Christ's death-like life and experience (so the cross) in today's life context where so many fragmentations and self-centered ideologies ruin the life of all people on the globe, the way to multiculturalism will be paved. Our mutual understanding about different cultures and religions will be enhanced, because the work of Christ's death-like experience will be a basis for a just global community. Put differently, Christ's death becomes a common denominator to all who wish to make a difference in the context of self-seeking power or glory, because the cross brings forth solidarity and humility.

Summary

Against the hegemonic unity in our thinking and habits, I prefer an ethic of diversity and solidarity to one of imposed unity. Paul's critique of various constructions of power and ideologies in the Greco-Roman world and in the Corinthian community aims at a world of diversity in which all people live their life of diversity. For the sake of this kind of diversity-driven larger community for all, Paul lived and walked the walk of a loving God to the end of the world. What I read in Paul's life story reflected in First Corinthians and elsewhere has to do with this vision of a world full of diversity and solidarity. Paul himself carries Christ-like marks on his body; yet he hopes for a better world for all "in Christ," which is not a boundary marker but a creative, struggling space. A challenging question for all Christians is: Do we live out the gospel of Christ, in the form of the radical message that we carry the death of Christ in our bodies? "What you sow does not come to life unless it dies" (1 Cor 15:36). This good news, the gospel of Christ, is God's "yes" to the world and all people, because God is not just the God of the Israelites but also of the Gentiles (Rom 3:29).

Today, God calls people to work for a livable, peaceful world full of diversity and differences. If we respond to such a call, it is to live as a "body" so that we may share cross-cultural common denominators with each other. Then, we can create more room for true dialogue between cultures within the struggling spaces of our co-dependent human life in diversity. Under the aegis of diversity, irresponsible individualism or relativism should not be condoned. Challenging the traditional vision of Christian life as a lonely journey on the part of one who leaves family and community for a heavenly city (Bunyan's *Pilgrim's Progress*), an ethic of diversity aims at a responsible living together in mutual care. Paul offers a vision of living in diversity, respecting differences, engaging the other with a self-critical awareness, and caring for the other in solidarity and for creation in wonder.

Notes

Introduction: The Price of Unity

1. The phrase *sōma christou* is translated as "body of Christ," but its meaning involves complexities due to its genitive construction. Is it subjective or objective? As this book progresses, issues involving *soma christou* will become clearer.

2. Detailed investigation about the ecclesiological organism approach to the body of Christ will appear in Chapter 3.

3. Margaret Mitchell, *Paul and the Rhetoric of Reconciliation: An Exegetical Investigation of the Language and Composition of 1 Corinthians* (Louisville: Westminster/John Knox, 1992), 20–64. See also C. K. Barrett, *A Commentary on the First Epistle to the Corinthians* (New York: Harper & Row, 1968), 65–68; 157–64, 266–70. See also Michelle V. Lee, *Paul, the Stoics, and the Body of Christ* (Cambridge, U.K.: Cambridge University Press, 2006), 105–52.

4. Mitchell, *Paul and the Rhetoric,* 20–64.

5. See Ernst Käsemann, *Perspectives on Paul,* trans., Margaret Kohl (Philadelphia: Fortress Press, 1971), 102–21. See also E. Schweizer, *The Church as the Body of Christ* (Richmond, 1964) 23–40; "The Church as the Missionary Body of Christ," *New Testament Studies* 8 (1961): 5.

6. Bernhard W. Anderson, "The Tower of Babel: Unity and Diversity in God's Creation," in *From Creation to the New Creation: Old Testament Perspectives* (Minneapolis: Augsburg Fortress Press, 1994), 165–78.

7. Cynthia M. Campbell, *A Multitude of Blessings: A Christian Approach to Religious Diversity* (Louisville: Westminster/John Knox, 2007), 21–41.

8. Jacques Derrida, "The Villanova Roundtable," in *Deconstruction in a Nutshell: A Conversation with Jacques Derrida,* John D. Caputo, ed. (New York: Fordham University Press, 1997), 12–15.

9. The ideology of unity often takes the form of unitary or unilateral imposition. For the concept or the role of ideology in contemporary society and culture, see Louis Althusser, *Essays on Ideology,* trans. Ben Brewster (New York: Monthly Review Press, 1971), 36; and see John B. Thomson, *Ideology and Modern Culture: Critical Social Theory in the Era of Mass Communication* (Stanford: Stanford University Press, 1990), 58.

10. James Hollingshead, *Household of Caesar and the Body of Christ: A Political Interpretation of the Letters from Paul* (Lanham: Univ. Press of America, 1998), 191, 205–9.

11. Neighboring disciplines such as new literary criticism and postcolonial theories have had a decisive impact on biblical studies in the way that traditional hermeneutics began to give way to a new paradigm of postmodern hermeneutics. See Antony Easthope, *Literary into Cultural Studies* (London and New York: Routledge, 1991), 19–25, and Fernando F. Segovia, *Decolonizing Biblical Studies: A View from the Margin* (Maryknoll and New York: Orbis Books, 2000), 3–50. See also Jacques Derrida, "Différance," in *Margins of Philosophy,* trans. Alan Bass (Chicago: The University of Chicago Press, 1982), 1–27; Jacques Derrida, *Of Grammatology*, trans. Gayatri Chakravorty Spivak (Baltimore: Johns Hopkins University Press, 1974), 9; and Jacques Derrida, *Negotiations: Interventions and Interviews, 1971–2001*, edited, translated, and with an introduction by Elizabeth Rottenberg (Stanford: Stanford University Press, 2002), 12.

12. Daniel Patte, "Can One Be Critical without Being Autobiographical? The Case of Romans 1:26-27" in *Autobiographical Biblical Criticism: Academic Border Crossings—A Hermeneutical Challenge*, ed. Ingrid Rosa Kitzberger (Leiden: Deo Publishing, 2003), 34–59. See also *Ethics of Biblical Interpretation: A Reevaluation* (Westminster/John Knox, 1995).

13. Paul Ricoeur, *Time and Narrative,* vol. 3 (Chicago: University of Chicago Press, 1988), 246.

14. To begin with, the neologism of *de(re)construction* refers to both theory and practice. The theme of deconstruction and reconstruction runs through the whole book and will become clear gradually. Suffice it to say now, deconstruction and reconstruction should take place continually; there is no sense of "being done once-and-for-all." Rather, the task always demands a new way of deconstruction and reconstruction. Deconstruction and reconstruction are mutually bound in service to community for all. Deconstruction itself is not a goal or a means to achieving reconstruction. As Derrida put it, "deconstruction is not a method or some tool that you apply to something from the outside. Deconstruction is something which happens and which happens inside." See Jacques Derrida, "The Villanova Roundtable," 9. See also his *Memoires: For Paul de Man,* trans. Cecile Lindsay, Jonathan Culler, and Eduardo Cadava (New York: Columbia University Press, 1986), 124. Rather, deconstruction already contains reconstruction and vice versa. Therefore, one should think of de(re)construction as an inseparable, ongoing work of both theory and practice.

15. Derrida coins the phrase "relationless relation" in expressing our relation to others, community, state, and the world. Derrida envisions the world of being different, relationless, but of relatedness due to relationless. This is a paradox but important in our imagination of the world of relations including our personal relationships with others. Derrida, "The Villanova Roundtable," 14.

16. Derrida, "The Villanova Roundtable," 13. See also Paul Ricoeur, *Oneself as Another*, trans. Kathleen Blamey (Chicago and London: The University of Chicago Press, 1992), 21–23.

17. Cartesianism promotes a perspective of dualism, reductionism, and positivism by which philosophical universalism could take root. In the end, "truth" is

the opposite of otherness and difference. See Bryan Turner, *The Body and Society: Explorations in Social Theory* (London and Thousand Oaks, Calif.: Sage Publications, 1996), 9–13. See also Walter Lowe, *Theology and Difference: The Wound of Reason* (Indianapolis: Indiana University Press, 1993), 74: ". . . the *question* of truth is more than a question: it is a reality. And it is a reality which has hold of *us.*" See also James S. Hans, *The Question of Value: Thinking through Nietzsche, Heidegger and Freud* (Carbondale: Southern Illinois University Press, 1989), 123–24; John D. Caputo, *Radical Hermeneutics: Repetition, Deconstruction, and the Hermeneutic Project* (Bloomington: Indiana University Press, 1987), 7.

18. Diversity is the uppermost issue for today's theological reflections and in biblical studies. Theodore Brelsford put it as "the irreducible diversity of human life in all its aspects; the existence of distinctively different races, cultures, communities, traditions, views, values, etc." See Theodore Brelsford, "Christological Tensions in a Pluralistic Environment: Managing the Challenges of Fostering and Sustaining both Identity and Openness," in *Religious Education* 90.02:174-89. See also Bernhard W. Anderson, "The Tower of Babel," in *From Creation to the New Creation: Old Testament Perspectives* (Minneapolis: Augsburg Fortress, 1994), 165–78.

19. Jacques Derrida, "The Villanova Roundtable," 13, and Emmanuel Lévinas, "Dialogue on Thinking-of-the-Other," in *Entre Nous: Thinking-of-the-Other*, trans. Michael B. Smith and Barbara Harshav (New York: Columbia Univ. Press, 1998) 204–5.

20. Douglas Knight, "The Ethics of Human Life in the Hebrew Bible," in *Justice and the Holy: Essays in Honor of Walter Harrelson,* ed. Douglas A. Knight and Peter J. Paris (Atlanta: Scholar Press, 1989), 82. Knight states that God is "the giver of life (Deut 30:19; Job 33:3), the fountain of life (Ps 36:9) and of living waters (Jer 2:13; 17:13), the preserver of life (Ps 64:1)."

21. Diogenes Laertius, *Lives of Eminent Philosophers*, trans. R. D. Hicks (Cambridge, Mass.: Harvard University Press, 2000), 6, 63. The used form is *cosmopolites* from which cosmopolitan is derived. The question is how or why Diogenes used such a term as cosmopolitan. If Laertius's writing is authentic, "cosmopolitan" originated with Diogenes. As I will show in Chapter 3, the voice of Diogenes the Cynic seems to decry all sorts of the hegemonic body politic that suppresses human dignity, equality, and freedom. Diogenes answered that the beautiful thing in the world is "freedom of speech" (*parrhēsia*) (6.69).

22. bell hooks, *Yearning: Race, Gender, and Cultural Politics* (Boston: South End Press, 1990), 149–52. I use the notion of "all" in my book similar to a gathering of all differentiations, not a gathering of the unified whole, totality, or any universalism.

23. For a brief history of Korea, see Daniel M. Davies, "The Impact of Christianity upon Korea, 1884–1910: Six Key American and Korean Figures," *Journal of Church and State* 36 (1994): 795–820.

24. Cristina Grenholm and Daniel Patte, "Overture: Reception, Critical Interpretations, and Scriptural Criticism," in *Reading Israel in Romans: Legitimacy and Plausibility of Divergent Interpretations*, ed. Cristina Grenholm and Daniel Patte (Harrisburg, Pa.: Trinity International Press, 2000), 1:1–54. See also James Aageson,

Written Also for Our Sake: Paul and the Art of Biblical Interpretation (Louisville: Westminster/John Knox, 1993), 3–18.

1. Community as "Body"

1. Michelle Lee, *Paul, the Stoics, and the Body of Christ*, 105. Lee argues that the Corinthians' identity in Christ is the basis of ethics.

2. W. D. Davies, *Paul and Rabbinic Judaism: Some Rabbinic Elements in Pauline Theology,* 4th ed. (Philadelphia: Fortress, 1980), 57.

3. Ibid. See also J. C. Beker, *The Triumph of God*, 70–71.

4. Patte, *Paul's Faith and the Power of the Gospel.* See also Beker, *The Triumph of God*, 70–71.

5. See Ehrensperger, "New Perspectives on Paul—No New Perspectives on Romans in Feminist Theology?" 227–58. See also Vincent Wimbush, "Reading Texts as Reading Ourselves: A Chapter in the History of African-American Biblical Interpretation," in *Reading from this Place*, vol.1, ed. Fernando F. Segovia and Mary Ann Tolbert (Minneapolis: Fortress Press, 1995), 95–108. See also Tolbert, "Reading for Liberation," in *Reading from this Place,* vol. 1. See also Ahn Byung-Mu, "Jesus and the Minjung in the Gospel of Mark," 85–104. See also Kwok Pui Lan, "Discovering the Bible in the Non-biblical world," 289–305.

6. Boyarin, *A Radical Jew: Paul and the Politics of Identity,* 181.

7. Ibid.

8. Baur, *Paul: His Life and Works*, 1–43; 61–65.

9. Ibid.

10. Derrida, "The Villanova Roundtable," 12–15. Derrida distances himself from all unity-oriented discourses or of mere multiplicity: "Pure unity or pure multiplicity—when there is only totality or unity and when there is only multiplicity or disassociation—is a synonym of death." Derrida, "The Villanova Roundtable," 13. Rather, he posits an identity of self-differentiation through radical thinking. After an interview with Derrida, John Caputo observes rightly about him: For Derrida, there is no "*Wesen* and no *telos* but only *différance*, no deep essence to keep things on course but a certain contingent assembly of unities subject always to a more radical open-endedness that constantly runs the risk of going adrift." Caputo continues: Derrida rejects "Hegel's notion of a dialectical unity-in-difference" because it is "archeoteleogical" and assumes higher principles or the Spirit. See Caputo, *Deconstruction in a Nutshell,* 117.

11. Ehrensperger, "New Perspectives on Paul—No New Perspectives on Romans in Feminist Theology?" 227–58.

12. Bultmann, *Theology of New Testament*, vol.1, 309.

13. Ibid., 49. See also *Christ and Israel: An Interpretation of Romans 9–11* (Philadelphia: Fortress Press, 1967), 3–22.

14. See Durkheim, *The Division of Labor in Society*, 76–115.

15. Ibid.

16. For the sociology of sect, see Saldarini, *Matthew's Christian-Jewish Community* and *Pharisees, Scribes and Sadducees in Palestinian Society.* For the sociology of knowledge, see Peter Berger, *The Social Construction of Reality,* 92–128. See also Peter Berger, *The Sacred Canopy*, 21–40.

For the functionalist approach, see Theissen, *Pauline Christianity,* 36–37, 96–99, 121–40.

17. Peter Berger and Thomas Luckmann, *The Social Construction of Reality,* 92–128. See also Peter Berger, *The Sacred Canopy,* 21–40.

18. Ibid.

19. Burke, "Paul's Role as 'Father' to his Corinthian 'Children,'" 107. See also Joubert, "Managing the Household," 213–23.

20. Bousset, *What is Religion?* 267, 269.

21. Troeltsch, *The Absoluteness of Christianity and the History of Religions,* 114.

22. Ibid., 117.

23. Bousset, *What is Religion?* 294.

24. Bousset, *Kyrios and Christos*, 46–55.

25. Bousset, *Kyrios*, 154.

26. Schuyler Brown, review in *Catholic Biblical Quarterly* 33 (02): 242–43. Glenn Hinson, review in *Review and Expositor* 68 (04): 548–49.

27. Theissen, *The Social Setting of Pauline Christianity*, 36–37, 96–99, 121–40.

28. Johannes Munck, *Paul and the Salvation of Mankind* (Richmond: John Knox Press, 1960). See also Oscar Cullmann, *Salvation in History*, tr. Sidney G. Sowers (New York: Harper & Row, 1967), 65; 19–83.

29. Douglas, *Purity and Danger,* 114–15. In contrast with Douglas, Fiorenza acknowledges the agency of women who opposed society's hierarchical, patriarchic voices in Pauline communities. Fiorenza, *In Memory of Her*, 79–80; and Fiorenza, "Rhetorical Situation and Historical Reconstruction in 1 Corinthians," 386–403. See also Wire, *The Corinthian Women Prophets,* 116–34. I agree with Fiorenza's reconstruction of women's voices as agency, but I do not agree with her view of Paul. I read Paul as egalitarian.

30. Meeks, *The First Urban Christians*, 74–75; 164–70.

31. King, "Feminist Theologies in Contemporary Contexts," 109. Regarding the fluidity of boundaries, see Bhabha, *The Location of Culture,* 34–35, 114–15.

32. Fiorenza, *In Memory of Her*, 79–80; Fiorenza, "Rhetorical Situation and Historical Reconstruction in 1 Corinthians," 386–403. See also Wire, *The Corinthian Women Prophets*, 116–34.

33. Brett, "Interpreting Ethnicity," 3–22.

34. Bhabha, *The Location of Culture*, 34–35, 114–15.

35. Tan Yak-Hwee, "Judging and Community in Romans," 39–62.

36. Ibid.

37. Ibid.

38. Bhabha, *The Location of Culture*, 34–35, 114–15. See also Nicole Wilkinson Duran and Derya Demirer, "1 Corinthians 11 in Christian and Muslim Dialogue," 451–54.

39. I will discuss the topic of new space or hybridity in chapter 4 when I address conceptions of "in Christ." I will consider the idea of "in Christ" in a specific way that it can be an active, intervening space.

40. Schweizer, *The Church as the Body of Christ*, 23–40 and his "The Church as the Missionary Body of Christ," 5. Bousset, *Kyrios and Christos*, 46–55; *What is Religion?* 267–69. See also Troeltsch, *The Absoluteness of Christianity*, 114.

41. Schweizer, *The Church as the Body of Christ*, 23–40. Robinson, *The Body*, 51. See also Cerfaux, *The Church in the Theology of St. Paul*, 274, 277. See also H. Schlier, *The Relevance of the New Testament* (New York: Herder and Herder, 1968), 22–25, and Wedderburn, "The Body of Christ and Related Concepts in 1 Corinthians," 74–96.

42. See Odell-Scott, *Paul's Critique of Theocracy,* 1–5.

43. Theissen, *Pauline Christianity*, 36–37, 96–99, 121–40; Martin, *The Corinthian Body*, 92–96.

44. Durkheim, *The Elementary Forms of Religious Life,* 44.

45. Lowe, *Theology and Difference*, 5. See also Metz, *Faith in History and Society*, 28–29.

46. Wainwright, "A Voice from the Margin," 132–53.

47. See Fiorenza, "Rhetorical Situation and Historical Reconstruction in 1 Corinthians," 386–403; *In Memory of Her*. See also Wire, *The Corinthian Women Prophets*, 116–34. Wire points out that Paul suppresses women Christians who radically proclaim their freedom in Christ.

48. Derrida, "The Villanova Roundtable," 15; Harink, *Paul among the Postliberals*, 242–48.

49. See J. Y. Lee, *Marginality: The Key to Multicultural Theology*, 29–76. Lee claims that multicultural theology should be based on a perspective of "in-both" and "in-beyond." See also Odell-Scott, *Paul's Critique of Theocracy*, 21–23.

50. I use "identity politics" here in the sense that scholars or practitioners of politics advocate one identity against the other by making distinctions between oppressors and the oppressed. See also McLaren, *Feminism, Foucault, and Embodied Subjectivity*, 1–17.

51. Derrida, "The Villanova Roundtable," 13–15. Derrida emphasizes self-differentiation of identity, culture, and community from itself and with others. The condition of being different is a basis of substantial community. The following quotation helps to clarify what he states: "Sometimes the struggles under the banner of cultural identity, national identity, linguistic identity, are noble fights. But at the same time the people who fight for their identity must pay attention to the fact that identity is not the self identity of a thing, this glass, for instance, this microphone, but implies a difference within identity. That is, the identity of a culture is a way of being different from itself; a culture is different from itself; language is different from itself; the person is different from itself. Once you take into account this

inner and other difference, then you pay attention to the other and you understand that fighting for your own identity is not exclusive of another identity, is open to another identity. And this prevents totalitarianism, nationalism, egocentrism, and so on" (p. 13).

52. Bhabha, *The Location of Culture*, 4, 114–15, 219, 242. Therefore, the newly conceived community is not a single community based on a single category.

53. Ibid. See also hooks, *Yearning*, 149–52; Frantz Fanon, *Black Skin, White Masks*, trans. Charles Lam Markmann (New York: Grove, 1967), 229, 230.

54. As it will become clearer, the "body of Christ" that I use is not a metaphorical organism but a "living" metaphor. The next chapters will deal with that issue in one way or another.

2. Community as the "Body of Christ"

1. Methodologically, we must understand the phrase "body of Christ" as a metaphor even when scholars such as Käsemann, Robinson, and others deny that it is a metaphor; thus simply rejecting the view that it is a specific kind of metaphor, namely a metaphor for an ecclesiological organism. Following Paul Ricoeur's definition in *The Rule of the Metaphor*, p. 7, saying that the "body of Christ" is a metaphor is not simply saying that the relationship of "something" (a community, a believer's life) to Christ is like the relationship between the church and his body (or vice versa). It also is saying that this relationship to Christ also is unlike the relationship between Christ and his body (or vice versa). Thus saying that "each of them is the body of Christ, in that each is the physical complement and extension of the one and the same Person and Life" (Robinson, *The Body*, 51), is still interpreting "body of Christ" as a metaphor—although not as a metaphor for an ecclesiological organism.

2. Jewett, *Paul's Anthropological Terms: A Study of Their Use in Conflict Settings*, 209–25.

3. Horsley, "1, 2 Corinthians." See also Horsley, *1 Corinthians*, 173. See Elliott, "Paul's Letters," 122–47.

4. Horsley, "Rhetoric and Empire—1 Corinthians," 72–102.

5. Theissen, *The Social Setting of Pauline Christianity*, 36–37, 96–99, 121–40. Martin, *The Corinthian Body*, 92–96.

6. Theissen, *Pauline Christianity,* 36–37, 96–99, 121–40; Martin, *The Corinthian Body,* 92–96. See also Martin, 94. Similarly, Martin views the body of Christ as a "benevolent patriarchalism." Ironically, Martin's reading of the "body of Christ" is ambivalent; Paul opposes the dominant society's ideology of a hierarchical "body" through body analogy (12:12-26) but accepts a hierarchical view of the body (church) as a given.

7. Neyrey, *Paul, in Other Words*, 116.

8. Douglas, *Purity and Danger*, 114–15.

9. Neyrey, *Paul, in Other Words*, 116.

10. See Mitchell, *Paul and the Rhetoric of Reconciliation*, 20–64. See also Barrett, *A Commentary on the First Epistle to the Corinthians*, 292–93.

11. See Mitchell, *Paul and the Rhetoric of Reconciliation*, 20–64. See also Barrett, *A Commentary on the First Epistle to the Corinthians*, 292–93. See also Dunn, "'The Body of Christ' in Paul," 146–62; and Dunn, *The Theology of Paul the Apostle*, 533–64. See Furnish, "Theology in 1 Corinthians," 59–89; Witherington, *Conflict and Community in Corinth,* 261.

12. See also Wanamaker, "A Rhetoric of Power: Ideology and 1 Corinthians 1–4," 119–22. From a rhetorical perspective, this constitutes a *topos* of concord (*peri homonoias*), which was a well-known *topos* among both ancient politicians and rhetoricians." See Castelli, *Imitating Paul: A Discourse of Power*, 15.

13. Mitchell, *Paul and the Rhetoric of Reconciliation*, 20–64.

14. Gundry, *Soma in Biblical Theology with Emphasis on Pauline Anthropology*, 232; Barrett, *A Commentary on the First Epistle to the Corinthians*, 287–92.

15. Gundry, *Soma in Biblical Theology*, 223–44.

16. Barrett, *A Commentary on the First Epistle to the Corinthians*, 42–49, 148–49, 292–93.

17. Robinson, *Corporate Personality in Ancient Israel*, 25–60.

18. Ibid., 27.

19. Davies, *Paul and Rabbinic Judaism*, 57.

20. Schweizer, "The Missionary Body of Christ," 5; "soma ktl," 1074–80.

21. Schweizer, *The Church as the Body of Christ*, 23–40.

22. Ibid.

23. Ibid.

24. Ernst Käsemann, *Perspectives on Paul*, 108–9.

25. Schweitzer, *The Mysticism of Paul the Apostle*, 293–333.

26. Ibid., 118.

27. Ibid., 297.

28. Ibid., 301.

29. Ibid.

30. Ibid., 302.

31. Ibid. References can be found: 1 Thess 4:3; Rom 6:6, 11, 13; 8:5, 12-14; 12:1; 1 Cor 6:20; 1 Cor 13; Gal 5:13-14.

32. Ibid.

33. Similarly, Wedderburn opposes the idea of the "body of Christ" as a metaphor for an ecclesiological organism because for him the cross is a basis of unity for believers in Christ. See Wedderburn, "The Body of Christ and Related Concepts in 1 Corinthians," 74–96. Cerfaux also rejects the view of a "social body" and emphasizes the "physical" "body of Christ." See Cerfaux, *The Church in the Theology of St Paul*, 274–77. He translates 1 Cor 12:27: "You are a body, a body which is that of Christ (dependent on him, and in which his life flows)."

34. Käsemann, *Perspectives on Paul*, 103–5.

35. Minear, *Images of the Church in the New*, 173ff.

36. Käsemann, *Exegetische Versuche und Besinnungen*, 1:16.

37. Käsemann, *Leib und Leib Christi: Eine Untersuchung zur paulinischen Begrifflichkeit*, 108, 184–85.

38. Ibid., 116.

39. Käsemann, *Perspectives on Paul*, 116–17.

40. Ibid., 117–18.

41. Ibid., 118.

42. Käsemann, *Perspectives on Paul*, 117.

43. Ibid., 103–17.

44. In this approach, Paul is viewed as a socially conservative, elite, Roman Stoic rhetorician, seeking peace and unity at the expense of diversity or differences in the community.

45. Odell-Scott, *Paul's Critique of Theocracy*, 7–13.

46. Sanders, "1 Corinthians," 294.

3. Community "in Christ"

1. Wedderburn, "Paul's Use of the Phrases 'in Christ' and 'with Christ,'" 83–97.

2. Bouttier, *En Christ*, 45.

3. Neugebauer, "Das Paulinische 'in Christo,'" 124–38.

4. Wedderburn criticizes Neugebauer's objectivistic approach that seeks to define "in Christ" by circumstances such as eschatological events and insists that "in Christ" is not the definition of such objective circumstances. For Wedderburn, the phrase "in Christ" defines "the circumstances in which something is or happens (objective genitive), and the circumstances which are thus defined may be the time, the place, the manner, etc." Wedderburn, "Paul's Use of the Phrases 'in Christ' and 'with Christ,'" 83–97.

5. See Dodd, *The Epistle of Paul to the Romans*, 87. See also Bultmann, *Theology of the New Testament,* 1:309.

6. See Schweitzer, *Mysticism*, 388. Similarly but with different reasons, Andrie du Toit insists that "in Christ" has both objective and subjective uses depending on its use in each letter. Under the title of "metaphorical local," he categorizes two sub-sets, which are "Christ as the realm of God's salvational presence" (Rom 3:24; 6:23; 8:2, 39; etc.) and "Christ/Lord as the realm of Christian's new existence." The latter again divides into two modes of indicative (Rom 6:11; 8:1; 1 Cor 1:2-5; 4:10; 11:1; 15:18, 22; 16:24, etc.) and imperative (Rom 9:1; 1 Cor 7:39; 9:1, 2; 15:31, 58; Gal 5:10). See also du Toit, "'In Christ,' 'in the Spirit' and Related Prepositional Phrases," 287–98.

7. Schweitzer, *Mysticism,* 380.

8. Käsemann, *Perspectives on Paul*, 102–21 and *Essays on New Testament Themes,* 129. See also Beker, *The Triumph of God*, 70–71. See also du Toit's "'In Christ,' 'in the Spirit' and Related Prepositional Phrases," 287–98; Schweitzer, *Mysticism*, 380.

9. There is a minority view that a woman needs only to stay within the community and not forget her Christian duties. Lightfoot, *Notes on the Epistles of Paul*, 225.

10. Tertullian *Against Marcion* 5.7; Cyprian *Testimony* 3.62; Jerome *Epistles* 123.5; Calvin *First Epistle* 168.

11. Collins, *First Corinthians,* 303. See also Fee, *The First Epistle to the Corinthians*, 356.

12. Odell-Scott, *Paul's Critique of Theocracy*, 89–90.

13. Bultmann, *Theology of the New Testament*, 1:311. See also Bornkamm, *Paul*, 155.

14. Barrett, *A Commentary on the First Epistle to the Corinthians*, 31. See also Conzelmann, *1 Corinthians*, 212–14. Conzelmann states that in the body of Christ (church), there are no differences (physical and social) and that unity determines parts.

15. Garcia, *Teaching in a Pluralistic Society*, 46.

16. Sibley, *Geographies of Exclusion*, 23–24; hooks, *Black Looks*, 167. Seminal texts of postcolonialism such as Edward Said's Orientalism and Frantz Fanon's *The Wretched of the Earth* concern Western imperialism and domination (social, political, cultural). Edward Said, *Orientalism* (New York: Vintage Books, 1979); Frantz Fanon, *Black Skin, White Masks*, trans. Charles Lam Markmann (New York, Grove Press, 1967), 229, 230. See also Gearon, "The Imagined Other," 98–106.

17. Mitchell, *Paul and the Rhetoric of Reconciliation*, 288.

18. For example, see Kelly Chong's survey on an ethnic congregation's sociological behavior in relation to its own identity and outside community: Chong, "What It Means to Be Christian," 259–87.

19. Paul Sampley reads "in the Lord," for example, as a strict boundary marker. See the notes in Sampley, *New Interpreter's Study Bible*, 2047. Widows should marry only fellow believers. However, in fact, there is another way to read this "in the Lord." What is required for a widow who remarries is not to distinguish who is "in Christ" and who is not; rather, the criteria or the challenge is whether one can commit one's life (and body) to the Lord.

20. See Williams, *Christ in You*, 110–15.

21. "In Christ" appears in 1 Corinthians as follows: 1:2 (those who are sanctified in Christ Jesus); 1:4 (God's grace in Christ Jesus); 1:30 (Christ is the source of our life in Christ Jesus: wisdom, righteousness, sanctification, and redemption); 3:1 (infants in Christ); 4:10 (you are wise "in Christ"); 4:15 (ten thousand guardians in Christ, but not the father); 4:17 (to remind you of my ways in Christ Jesus); 15:18 (those who have died in Christ have perished); 15:19 (If for this life only we have hoped in Christ); 15:22 (For as all die in Adam, so all will be made alive in Christ); 15:31 (I die every day! That is as certain, brothers and sisters, as my boasting of you—a boast that I make in Christ Jesus our Lord; 16:24 (My love be with all of you in Christ Jesus).

22. Bhabha, *The Location of Culture*, 7.

23. Odell-Scott, *Paul's Critique of Theocracy*, 21–23. Odell-Scott deconstructs the hierarchy and power claims in Corinthians. See also Braxton, *No Longer Slaves*, 95.

24. Mark Taylor rightly grasps the difficulty of postmodernity: "postmodern trilemma" in which he includes tradition/identity (keep), plurality (celebrate), and domination (resist). See Taylor, *Remembering Esperanza*, 31.

25. Sally R. Munt, "Framing Intelligibility, Identity, and Selfhood," http://recon struction.eserver.org/023/munt.htm.

26. Ernest Becker points out the contemporary problem of "denial of death": "The root of humanly caused evil is not man's animal nature, not territorial aggression, or innate selfishness, but our need to gain self-esteem, deny our mortality, and achieve a heroic self-image." Ernst Becker, *The Denial of Death* (New York: Free Press, 1973), xii.

27. Odell-Scott, *Paul's Critique of Theocracy*, 161.

28. Ibid., 17. See also Agamben, *Homo sacer*, 120. Agamben problematizes the state of exception that can be so destructive with the justification of power.

29. Welborn argues that Paul's acceptance of the role of a fool has to do with the fool's role in the mime of the popular theater. In other words, Paul gladly accepts his role as such being associated with the image of the cross to protest against injustices. Welborn, *Paul, the Fool of Christ*, 99–101.

30. These opponents are probably from Christ's own family or close followers of Jesus. See Odell-Scott, *Paul's Critique of Theocracy*, 47.

31. Welborn, *Paul, the Fool of Christ*, 99–101.

32. The central symbol in 1 Corinthians is Christ crucified—the symbol of weakness and the power of God (1:18–2:5). Paul repeatedly emphasizes the preaching of Christ crucified (1:23; 2:2) and his "ways in Christ Jesus" (4:17); he dies every day with boasting of the death of Christ (15:31).

33. Yagi suggests that believers can have Christ's life/experience/views through living the Christ. Yagi, "*I* in the Words of Jesus," 330–51.

34. Welborn, *Paul, the Fool of Christ*, 99–101. See also Hengel, *Crucifixion,* 1–10. For an experience of shame and liminality, see Agamben, *Remnants of Auschwitz,* 87–135.

35. From this perspective of radical participation with those who suffer like Christ, Mel Gibson's movie, *The Passion of the Christ,* posits no ethical, participatory implications for Christians to be engaged in the violence that is rampant in the world today. See Kim, "Jesus' Death in Context."

36. See Butting, "Pauline Variations on Genesis 2:24." Baptism can be understood as dying with Christ; Odell-Scott, *Paul's Critique of Theocracy,* 22. See also Liddell, *Greek English Lexicon,* 305–6. *Baptizo* means quite literally 'to dip,' 'to immerse,' 'to bury' in a liquid; 'dipping cloth in dye.'" Odell-Scott put it: "mistakenly, *baptizo* came to be understood in the hermeneutical tradition of the institutional church as a ritual cleansing which purifies the person and signifies the 'ENTRY' of the person being 'baptized' into the body of Christ."

37. Derrida, "Différance," 396–420.

38. Grosz, *Space, Time, and Perversion,* 92, 214.

39. Bhabha, *The Location of Culture,* 4, 114–15, 219, 242. Bhabha uses the terms "third space," "being in the beyond," and "in-between space" to express a resistant

and creative space. In addition, I emphasize "third" as non-belonging space and time that no person or group dominates. Therefore, Trinh T. Minh-ha points out the importance of resistance in this struggle to find subjectivity. See Minh-ha, "Cotton and Iron," 327–36.

40. Lefebvre, *The Production of Space,* 6, 11, 59, 73. Lefebvre corrects the Kantian ideals of consciousness by the notion of the lived space and the social space. Pierre Bourdieu's concept of *habitus* points to a kind of space-body in which culture is inscribed. See Bourdieu, *An Invitation to Reflexive Sociology,* 133.

41. See Arai, "Religious Education in Christ-with-Culture," 222–37, and see also Brelsford, "Christological Tensions in a Pluralistic Environment," 174–89. See also Stendahl, "Religious Pluralism and the Claim to Uniqueness," 181–83.

4. The Body Politic and the Body of Christ

1. Michelle Lee, *Paul the Stoics, and the Body of Christ,* 105–52. See also Mitchell, *Paul and the Rhetoric of Reconciliation,* 20–64; Barrett, *Paul and the Corinthians,* 65–68, 157–64, 266–70.

2. The body politic of the hegemonic body has deep roots in Plato's Republic in which philosophers rule the state with reason (aristocracy: "the government of the best"). Plato's view of soul is also hierarchical because it presupposes the rule of aristocracy. See *Respublica,* 439C–441B; 543.

3. I take seriously Plato's hierarchical, dualistic worldview that influenced the interpretation of history and theology. For instance, Plato's dualism between pure ideas and the current cosmos and between the body and the soul carries over to Newton's (1642–1727) mechanical worldview of body and nature and to Descartes's (1596–1650) ontological dualism between mind and matter. Finally, the Reformation takes on rationalism, devaluing rituals, emotions, and feelings. See Frederik B. O. Nel, "An Ecological Approach to the Quest for New Horizons in the Christian View of Sexuality," in *Religion and Sexuality,* ed. Michael Hayes, Wendy Porter, and David Tombs (Sheffield, U.K.: Sheffield Academic, 1998), 380–404.

4. Though Plato sets a radical division between the body (*soma*) and the soul (*psyche*), his dualism is different from the Cartesian ontological dichotomy between matter and non-matter, body and spirit (mind). For Plato, even the soul is of matter (three distinct forms of soul). See Martin, 3–37.

5. *Timaeus,* 40A: "And these Forms are four—one the heavenly kind of gods (i.e., the stars); another the winged kind which traverses the air; thirdly, the class which inhabits the waters; and fourthly, that which goes on foot on dry land." Quoted from a trans. by R. G. Bury (Cambridge, Mass.: Harvard University Press, 1929).

6. Plato *Respublica* 439C–441B.

7. Ibid., 370A–B.

8. *Timaeus,* 44D; 90A, B.

9. Ibid., 42B; *Leges* 781A.

10. Plato, *Respublica,* 469B–471C.

11. Ioan P. Culianu, "Introduction: The Body Reexamined," in *Religious Reflection on the Human Body* (Bloomington: Indiana University Press, 1995), 1–18. See also Plato, *Thraede*, 209.

12. Martin, *The Corinthian Body*, 32.

13. Aristotle, *Politica* 1260a13.

14. Alexander of Aphrodisias, *Mixt.* 223.25, 224.14; Plutarch, *Comm. not.* 1085C–D; *Stoic. Rep.* 1053F, 1054A.

15. Manilius, *Astronomica* 1.247–54; Manilius goes on to say further: "the entire universe is alive in the mutual concord of its elements." Manilius, 2.63–68.

16. Diogenes Laertius, 7.139; Sextus Empiricus, *Adversus mathematicos* 9.130; Philodemus, *De Pietate* c.11 (SVF 2.1076).

17. Laertius, 7.138–9.

18. Seneca, *De beneficiis* 1.10.3–4; 4.27.1–3.

19. Martin, *The Corinthian Body*, 30.

20. Mitchell, *Paul and the Rhetoric of Reconciliation*, 157–64. See also Martin, 38–46. References to the society as a body can be found in the speeches of Aristides and Dio Chrysostom. Aristides, *Or.* 17.9; 23.31, 61; 24.16–18, 38–39; 26.43; Dio Chrysostom, *Disc.* 17.19; 34.18, 20, 22; 38.11–12; 39.5; 41.9.

21. Epictetus, *Dissertationes* 4.1.3.

22. Cicero, *De finibus* 1.18.61.

23. Ibid.

24. Interestingly enough, this internalizing attitude of a moral view has a resonance with Plato's view that the rational part of the soul controls the lower parts of the soul. *Respublica* 431A.

25. Mitchell, *Paul and the Rhetoric of Reconciliation*, part 3, passim. See also Martin, *The Corinthian Body*, 38–68, 92–96. These scholars see this organism metaphor as a dominant political discourse that advocates concord (or group harmony). For more about political discourse of concord, order, and unity, see also Dio Chrysostom *Discourses* 34.19; 38.11–14; 39.5; Aristides, *Orations* 23.40, 53, 73, 75; 24.47.

26. Livy, *History of Rome* 2.32.8–12.

27. See Augustus's own descriptions of his achievements in *Res Gestae Divi August,* trans. Brunt and Moore, 18–37.

28. For example, Augustus brags about his rule of peace: "I made the sea peaceful and freed it of pirates. In that war I captured about 30,000 slaves who had escaped from their masters and taken up arms against the republic, and I handed them over to their masters for punishment." See *Res Gestae*, 31. Klauck observes that the imperial cult serves as a symbolic tool to stabilize "the structure of power, in which the ruler and his subjects had their established positions." Klauck, *The Religious Context of Early Christianity*, 327.

29. Laertius, 6.20–81. See also Klauck, *The Religious Context of Early Christianity,* 378.

30. Laertius, 6.20–81. Lucian also says there are many Cynics: "The city swarms with these vermin, particularly those who profess the tenets of Diogenes, Antithenes, and Crates."

31. Foucault, "The Cynic Philosophers and Their Techniques." http://www.foucault.info/documents/parrhesiasts/foucault.diogenes.en.html.

32. Ibid. See also McLaren, *Feminism*, 152. See also Downing, *Cynics, Paul and the Pauline Churches,* 2:1–25.

33. Foucault, "Parrhesia and the Crisis of Democratic Institutions." http://www.foucault.info/documents/parrhesia/foucault.DT3.democracy.en.html. See also McLaren, Feminism, 145–64.

34. Laertius, 6.63.

35. Welborn, *Paul, the Fool of Christ*, 99–101.

36. Varro, *Ling. Lat.* 5.25.

37. Horace, *Satires* 1.8.8–13.

38. Juvenal, *Satires* 14.77–78.

39. Chariton, *Chaireas and Callirhoe,* 4.2.

40. See Eric Segal, *Roman Laughter: The Comedy of Plautus* (London: Oxford University Press, 1987), 137–69.

41. Josephus, *Jewish Antiquities* 13.380–83 and *Jewish War*, 5.449–51.

42. Josephus, *Jewish War* 7.203.

43. Philo, *Falccus* 84–85.

44. Tacitus, *Annales* 15.44.4

45. Jewett, *Paul the Apostle to America*, 3–31.

46. For example, E. Earle Ellis conceives of Christ crucified mainly as a theological category without relating it to the experience of the poor or slaves. Ellis, "Christ Crucified," in *Reconciliation and Hope*, 69–75.

47. Ehrensperger, "New Perspectives on Paul," 227–58.

48. Jewett, "The Corruption and Redemption of Creation," 25–46.

49. Louis Althusser, "Ideology and Ideology State Apparatuses,' in *idem, Lenin and Philosophy and Other Essays*, trans. Ben Brewster, (New York: Monthly Review Press, 1971), 155–62. I use Althusser's notion of ideology that includes an imaginary relation to the real world. For specific cases of conflicts, see C.K. Barrett, "Sectarian Diversity at Corinth," in *Paul and the Corinthians: Studies on a Community in Conflict*, eds. Trevor J. Burke and J. Keith Elliott (Leiden: Brill, 2003). See also C. K. Robertson, *Conflict in Corinth: Redefining the system,* (New York: P. Lang, 2001), 10.

50. William Baird, "'One against the Other': Intra-church Conflict in 1 Corinthians" in eds. Robert T. Fortna and Beverly R. Gaventa, *The Conversation Continues: Studies in Paul and John* (Nashville: Abingdon Press, 1990), 116–36.

51. See Sandra H. Polaski, *Paul and the Discourse of Power* (Sheffield: Sheffield Academic Press, 1999), 23–51. See also Elizabeth A. Castelli, *Imitating Paul*, 21–33.

52. Scholars who do not consider the Christ party as a possible faction include Hans Dieter Betz and Margaret Mitchell, both of whom view the Christ party as the real body of Christ. See Betz and Mitchell, "1 Corinthians," 1141.

53. Odell-Scott, *Paul's Critique of Theocracy*, 33.

54. Ibid., 40–43.

55. Ibid. *Merizō* conveys the sense of to divide as in to separate, but it is more than that; it conveys a sense of distribution, dealing out, apportioning of something to someone (1 Cor 1:13; 7:17, 33-4; 2 Cor 12:13; Rom 12:3). In contrast, *schizō* conveys a sense of to divide.

56. Ibid., 63.

57. Ibid., 54–55.

58. Odell-Scott relates the Christ party to James, the brother of Jesus. I think, from an ideological point of view, the Christ party seems to come from various constructions of power in the name of Christ. The James connection or the Jerusalem connection could be part of that. Odell-Scott, *Paul's Critique of Theocracy*, 47.

59. Ibid.

60. Conzelmann, *1 Corinthians*, 111.

61. Mitchell, *Paul and the Rhetoric of Reconciliation*, 120 (emphasis added).

62. Neyrey, *Paul, in Other Words*, 115.

63. Ernst Käsemann, *Essays on New Testament Themes* (London: SCM, 1964), 129.

64. Ibid., 130.

65. Horsley, "'How Can Some of You Say That There Is No Resurrection of the Dead?'" 203–31.

66. Bassler, "1 Corinthians," 413.

67. Peter Brown, *Society and Body*, 21–22.

68. Odell-Scott, *Paul's Critique of Theocracy*, 176.

69. Braxton, *The Tyranny of Resolution*, 220–34.

70. Sanders, "1 Corinthians," 294.

71. Barrett, *A Commentary on the First Epistle to the Corinthians*, 200. Barrett sees chapter 9 as the apostolic defense.

72. Conzelmann, 151. Conzelmann finds a new theme in chapter 9, which is the apostleship of Paul.

73. Willis, "An Apostolic Apology?" 33.

74. Nasuti, "The Woes of the Prophets and the Rights of the Apostle," 246–64. Nasuti sees the thematic continuance between chapter 8 and chapter 9 in terms of the correct use of liberty.

75. Malina and Rohrbaugh, *Commentary on the Synoptic Gospels*, 388. Malina and Rohrbaugh describe this patronage system as "socially fixed relations of generalized reciprocity between social unequals in which a lower-status person in need (client) has his needs met by having recourse for favors to a higher-status, well-situated person (patron). By being granted the favor, the client implicitly promises to pay back the patron. . . . The client relates to the patron as to a superior and more powerful kinsman, while the patron looks after his clients as he does his dependents."

76. Myers, "Balancing Abundance and Need."

77. Polaski, *Paul and the Discourse of Power*, 104.

78. Myers, "Balancing Abundance and Need."

79. Hanson and Oakman, *Palestine in the Time of Jesus*, 72.

80. Wire, *The Corinthian Women Prophets*, 220–23. She gives an overview of recent scholarly interpretations about the issue of a woman's head covering.

81. Barrett, *A Commentary on the First Epistle to the Corinthians*, 249–51. See also Conzelmann, *1 Corinthians*, 186, 191. O'Conner-Murphy, "1 Corinthians 11:2-16 Once Again," 265–74. O'Conner-Murphy sees the Corinthian problem limited to the specific behavior of "how they dressed their hair," and Paul argues for gender difference, not a subordination of women.

82. Bassler, "1 Corinthians," 416–17. Wire, *The Corinthian Women Prophets*, 130–31.

83. Schüssler Fiorenza, *In Memory of Her*, 233.

84. Trompf, "On Attitudes toward Women in Paul and Paulinist Literature," 196–215. See also Walker, "1 Corinthians and Paul's Views regarding Women," 94–110, both of whom insist that 11:2(3)-16 is an interpolation.

85. Odell-Scott, *Paul's Critique of Theocracy*, 168–72. See also Patte, *Paul's Faith and the Power of the Gospel*, 232–41, 339–41.

86. Odell-Scott, *Paul's Critique of Theocracy*, 168–72; Odell-Scott, "Let the Women Speak in Church," 90–93. See also his "In Defense of an Egalitarian Interpretation of 1 Cor 14:34-36," 100–103.

87. Witherington notes that the normal practice at Roman symposia (notorious for turning into drunken orgies) was "to rank one's guests in terms of social status, with those of higher status eating with the host in the dining room and others eating elsewhere and getting poorer food." Ben Witherington, *Conflict and Community*, 241. See also Myers, "Balancing Abundance and Need."

88. Myers, "Balancing Abundance and Need."

89. Theissen, *Pauline Christianity*, 36–37, 96–99, 121–40. Martin, *The Corinthian Body*, 92–96.

90. Theissen, *Pauline Christianity*, 36–37, 96–99, 121–40.

91. Schüssler Fiorenza, "Rhetorical Situation and Historical Reconstruction," 386–403.

92. Horsley, "Spiritual Elitism in Corinth," 203–31.

93. Ibid.

94. Becker, *The Denial of Death*, xii.

5. The Life of the "Body of Christ" in 1 Corinthians

1. Rom 6:11, 23; 8:1, 10; 12:5; 15:17; 16:3, 7, 9–10; 1 Cor 1:30; 3:1; 4:10, 15, 17; 15:18, 22; 16:24; 2 Cor 1:21; 2:14, 17; 3:14; 5:17, 19; 12:2, 19; Gal 1:22; 2:4, 16; 3:14, 26, 28; 5:6; Phil 1:1, 26, 29; 2:1, 5; 3:3, 9, 14; 4:7, 19, 21; 1 Thess 2:14; 4:16; 5:18; Phlm 1:8, 20, 23.

2. In the Deutero-Pauline letters, there is a strong sense of the body of Christ as an organism. For example, there are verses related to this ecclesiological organism: "reconciliation in *one* body" (Eph 2:16), "members of the *same* body" (Eph 3:6), "*one* body and *one* Spirit" (Eph 4:4), "body's growth" (Eph 4:16), "members of *his* body"

(Eph 5:30), and "called in the *one* body" (Col 3:15). The church as an institution (organism) is equal to the body of Christ whose head is Christ (Eph 4:12; 5:23; Col 1:18, 24; 2:19).

3. In the seven Pauline letters, "body" (*sōma*, excluding *sarkos* or *melos*) occurs eighty-three times among which 63 percent (fifty-two times) occur in 1 Corinthians only (1 Cor 5:3; 6:13, 15-16, 18-20; 7:4, 34; 9:27; 10:16f; 11:24, 27, 29; 12:12-20, 22, 24-25, 27; 13:3; 15:35, 37-38, 40, 44, 53-54). If we include twelve occurrences in 2 Corinthians, 1 and 2 Corinthians together account for 77 percent of the appearances of the term "body." The additional occurrences are thirteen times in Romans, one time in Galatians, three times in Philemon, and two times in 1 Thessalonians. Although this percentage does not necessarily show the importance of the concept of the "body" in each letter, the heavy use of this term in 1 Corinthians (fifty-two times out of eighty-three) suggests that there is something urgent about the "body" in this letter. That urgency can be understood from Paul's exhortation according to which the Corinthians should live Christ in their bodies to honor the weak and the marginalized.

4. The sense of physical body appears throughout the Pauline and Deutero-Pauline letters: Rom 1:24; 4:19; 2 Cor 5:6-8; 12:2-3; 7:5; Eph 5:28-29; Col 1:22; 2:5, 11; Heb 3:17; 9:10.

5. Conzelmann, *1 Corinthians*, 97–98. Barrett, *First Corinthians*, 126. Ernst Käsemann, "Sentences of Holy Law in the New Testament," in *New Testament Questions of Today* (Philadelphia: Fortress Press, 1969), 66–81.

6. This notion of "holistic body" dedicated to God appears in Romans: "members" as instruments of wickedness or of righteousness (6:13), "members" for sanctification (6:19), live by the Spirit or put to death the deeds of the body (8:10-11, 13), as a living sacrifice (12:1). In Philippians, Paul identifies the sinful and spiritual body: "the body of our humiliation" and "it may be conformed to the body of his glory, by the power that also enables him to make all things subject to himself" (2 Cor 3:21).

7. Conzelmann, *1 Corinthians*, 111.

8. Ibid., 111, note 21.

9. Mitchell, *Paul and the Rhetoric of Reconciliation*, 118–21.

10. In Pauline letters, one can find a sense of the Christic body—to live and die like Christ. In Romans, there is a consistent theme of this Christic body, e.g., "died to the law through the body of Christ" (Rom 7:4). Members embody Christ in their bodies by imitating Christ's faithfulness (Rom 3:22). Furthermore, the "body of Christ" in Rom 7:4 can be translated as Christic body (attributive genitive); as "body of sin" (Rom 6:6) can mean "sinful body." Galatians also has a strong sense of the Christic embodiment: "from now on, let no one make trouble for me; for I carry the marks of Jesus branded on my body" (Gal 6:17). With flesh (*sarx*) interchangeable with body (*sōma*), the idea of Christic body is also clear in Gal 2:20: "it is no longer I who live, but it is Christ who lives in me. And the life I now live in the flesh I live by faith in the Son of God, who loved me and gave himself for me." See also 2 Cor 4:10: "always carrying in the body the death of Jesus, so that the life of Jesus may also be made visible in our bodies."

11. In 1 Corinthians, the body of Christ is shared in the sense that believers participate in the work of Christ: "a sharing of the blood and the body of Christ" (10:16-17); "my body for you" (11:24); "the importance of Christ's sacrifice" (11:27, 29); "body analogy *with Christ*" (12:12); "act of baptism and drinking" (12:13); and "body analogy pointing to the attitudes of Christic body" (12:14-26).

12. For example, Gordon Fee takes it as possessive genitive. Fee, *God's Empowering Presence*, 188.

13. Pauline theology can be understood from the perspective of the marginalized as promoting the democratic and egalitarian body politic, with no partiality based on sex, gender, ethnicity, and class (Gal 3:28). See Downing, *Cynics, Paul, and the Pauline Churches,* 11–22; Braxton, *No Longer Slaves,* 94–95.

14. For two-step ethics, see Fee, "Toward a Theology of 1 Corinthians."

15. Patte, *The Religious Dimensions of Biblical Texts*, 141–58. Patte presents in detail the two following examples.

16. See Patte, *Structural Exegesis*, 9–22. See also his systematic analysis of the Gospel of Matthew using this principle; Patte, *The Gospel according to Matthew*.

17. See scholarly approaches to the interpretation of the body of Christ in Chapter 2. Mitchell is a typical example of reading the body of Christ in terms of the Greco-Roman rhetoric of social unity (*homonoia*).

18. As Odell-Scott also suggests; see Odell-Scott, *Paul's Critique of Theocracy*, 125.

19. The New Jerusalem Bible appropriately translates, "called you to be partners with his Son Jesus Christ our Lord."

20. Much would need to be said about the relationship between 11:2-16 and 11:17-34, as well as between 11:2-16 and 6:12-20. But for our present purpose, it is enough to focus on the primary inverted parallelisms between Ax (5:1-13) and A'x' (11:17-34) and the center of the chiastic figurative structure C (9:1-22).

21. Victor Furnish subdivides the letter as follows: 1:18–2:16; 12:4–13:3; 15. The fundamental difference with Furnish is that, for me, "body" does not function as a metaphor for an ecclesiological organism. See Furnish, "Theology in 1 Corinthians," 59–89. See also Furnish, *The Theology of the First Letter to the Corinthians,* 15–18.

22. Hollingshead, *Household of Caesar and the Body of Christ*, 208: "Paul's ethic is driven by the idea of giving up authority or power for the sake of others" (Rom 8:35-37). See also Alexandra R. Brown, *The Cross and Human Transformation*, 22–23.

23. James H. Cone, *The Spirituals and the Blues: An Interpretation* (New York: Seabury, 1972), 54. See also Kelly Brown Douglas, *The Black Christ* (Maryknoll, N.Y.: Orbis, 1994), 20–23.

24. Janssen, "Bodily Resurrection (1 Cor 15)?" 61–78.

25. Sölle, "Der Mensch zwischen Geist und Materie," 35.

26. A perspective of community can be understood as the opposite of individualism. Individualism can be "defined in a way that an individual is capable of anything apart from community, and precedes community or society as a whole . . . such folk owe no man anything and hardly expect anything from anybody. They form the

habit of thinking of themselves in isolation and imagine that their whole destiny is in their hands" (Bellah, *Habits of the Heart*, 37).

27. Paul uses faith, hope, and love at the same time in other places: "your work of faith and labor of love and steadfastness of hope in our Lord Jesus Christ" (1 Thess 1:3); "... your faith in Christ Jesus and of the love which you have ... of the hope laid up for you in heaven" (Col 1:4). In Paul's mind, faith, hope, and love should work together in Christian community.

28. Patte, *Paul's Faith*, 232–41. Daniel Patte emphasizes the typological aspects of faith that have to do with Paul's conviction of faith and with ours as well.

29. In my own translation of 1 Cor 13:4-7, I show aspects of the verb: "Love waits patiently and is kind; love does not envy; love does not boast itself, is not puffed up; does not behave rudely, does not seek its own, is not irritable, thinks no evil; does not rejoice at wrong, but rejoices in the truth; love protects (covers) all things, believes all things, hopes all things, endures all things."

30. This reading is based on a forensic understanding of God's love and salvation. Proponents of this reading are Luther, Bultmann, and Nygren, for example. Nygren, *Agape and Eros*, 21–56. Jeanrond, "Love," in *The Oxford Companion to Christian Thought*, 395–97.

31. There is a reading that synthesizes *agapē* and *erōs*, with a moderate view of God's love and a human's love. See Johnson, "Christian Perfection as Love for God," 97–113.

32. *Makrothymeō* (present, active, indicative, "wait patiently"); *chrēsteuomai* (present, middle, indicative, "to be good and kind"); *zeloō* (present, active, indicative, "to rival"); *perpereuomai* (to boast oneself); *physioō* (present, passive, indicative, "to puff up").

33. Conzelmann, *1 Corinthians*, 217–31. Barrett, *First Corinthians*, 297, 299.

34. This reading, more or less, is based on Jewish, Catholic, and Kierkegaardian views of love. See Jeanrond, "Love," 396.

35. Regarding two-step ethics, see Furnish, "Belonging to Christ," 145–57.

36. Papanikolaou, *"Person, Kenosis and Abuse,* 41–65. See also Hampson, *"On Autonomy and Heteronomy,"* 1–16; Coakley, *"Kenosis* and Subversion," 82–111.

37. Hampson, "On Autonomy and Heteronomy," 1–16

38. Jeanrond, "Love," 395–97.

39. Patte, *Paul's Faith*, 232–41.

40. Ibid.

41. Typological thinking has its origin in early Jewish apocalyptists and Qumran and was developed from the 2nd to the 4th centuries.

42. Wire, *The Corinthian Women Prophets*, 116–34. Fiorenza, "Rhetorical Situation and Historical Reconstruction in 1 Corinthians," 386–403.

43. Odell-Scott, "Let the Women Speak in Church: An Egalitarian Interpretation of First Corinthians 14:33b-36," in *Biblical Theology Bulletin* 13.3 (1983): 90–93; "In Defense of an Egalitarian Interpretation of First Corinthians 14:34-36: A Reply to Murphy-O'Connor's Critique," in BTB 17.3 (July 1987), 68–74; and "Editor's Dilemma," BTB 30.2 (2000): 68–74.

44. The use of body imagery with nature (15:42-44) can be an expression of Paul's theology of death and resurrection.

45. The language of death and resurrection can be understood in a political context where bodies are broken and humiliated. Body is a site for protest in that context. See Gager, "Body Symbols and Social Reality," 345–63. See also Setzer, "Resurrection of the Dead as Symbol and Strategy," 65–95.

46. Gager, "Body Symbols and Social Reality," 345–63.

47. Sobrino, *Christ the Liberator*, 47–53.

48. Resurrection of the flesh does not appear in the NT but resurrection of the dead does (Matt 22:31; Luke 20:35; Acts 4:2; 17:32; 23:6; 24:21; 26:23; Rom 1:4; 1 Cor 15:12, 13, 21; Heb 6:2; 1 Pet 1:3). Church fathers such as Clement, Ignatius, *Didache*, Polycarp, Justin Martyr, Irenaeus, and Tertullian also spoke of the resurrection of the flesh. Origen, however, denied the resurrection of the corporeality. Reformers such as Luther shared a similar understanding.

49. Janssen, "Bodily Resurrection," 61–78. See also Braxton, *The Tyranny of Resolution*, 186–209.

50. Janssen, "Bodily Resurrection," 61–78.

51. Janssen, "Bodily Resurrection," 61–78.

52. This reading of resurrection was already anticipated by Karl Barth and Rudolf Bultmann. For Barth, resurrection is not yet realized but it is part of reality already. Resurrection is the object of hope and faith, and the death of the body is necessary in order to experience resurrection in the future (Barth, *The Resurrection of the Dead*, 125–213). Bultmann, however, understands it in present terms; something is happening now in the world, not as a future reality from which present reality is separated by *krisis* or judgment, but rather as a present reality, which can be experienced individually or existentially. Bultmann continues to say that, "when Paul speaks of the resurrection of the dead, it is clear that he means to speak of *us*, of our reality, of our existence, of a reality in which *we* stand" (Bultmann, *Faith and Understanding*, 81).

In terms of Bultmann's emphasis on the present realization of resurrection, his view is similar to mine, but his view is also very different from mine in that for him, the resurrection message validates the individualism of an existential reading. In other words, for Bultmann, resurrection is an individual event and existence, remote from the everyday political, economic, and downtrodden life of ordinary people. In contrast, Barth allows room for engaging justice in this world where resurrection is not yet available. Resurrection must come partially in this world through the struggle of living between now and then. However, Barth fails to elaborate on the bodiliness of resurrection because of his conception of death as a turning point, which entails "the tendency to devalue bodily life" (Janssen, "Bodily Resurrection," 61–78). In this regard, Dorothee Sölle's critique is valid: "resurrection requires a place where the contradictions of life are resolved . . . a place that supplies the strength to confront the tension between our experience of the present and the promise of life, in order that this tension may not shatter us" (Sölle, "Der Mensch zwischen Geist und

Materie," 18). "Bodiliness" includes the physical or spiritual limitedness as humans and specific cases of the oppressed body.

53. Janssen, "Bodily Resurrection," 32. The concept of 'body,' on which Paul builds this positive view of the creaturely condition, and which is the key to an understanding of resurrection that is visible in 1 Corinthians 15.

6. Practicing the Diversity of Christ's Body

1. Campbell, *A Multitude of Blessings* (Louisville: W/JKP, 2007), 27. See also Hiebert, *Toppling the Tower*, 10. *Balal* also can mean "mixed" in the sense that priests mix ingredients used in offerings.

2. Campbell, *A Multitude of Blessings*, 23–41.

3. Ibid.

4. Ibid.

5. Warrior, "A Native American Perspective," 287–95.

6. Grenholm and Patte, "Overture: Reception, Critical Interpretations, and Scriptural Criticism."

7. Derrida, "The Villanova Roundtable," 13. Emmanuel Levinas, "Dialogue on Thinking-of-the-Other," in *Entre Nous: Thinking of the Other*, trans. Michael B. Smith and Barbara Harshav (New York: Columbia, 1998), 204–5.

8. Ricoeur's twofold identity ipse has the character of changing over time; self has complexity and differences in that regard, and it should be evaluated as an ongoing dialogue partner. Ricoeur, *Oneself as Another*.

9. Derrida, "The Villanova Roundtable," 12–15.

10. Barclay, "Neither Jew nor Greek," 213.

11. Bassler, *Navigating Paul*, 4–5.

Bibliography

Agamben, Giorgio. *Homo Sacer: Sovereign Power and Bare Life.* Translated by Daniel Heller-Roazen. Stanford: Stanford University Press, 1998.

———. *Remnants of Auschwitz: The Witness and the Archive.* Translated by Daniel Heller-Roazen, New York: Zone Books, 1999.

Ahn, Byung-Mu. "Jesus and the Minjung in the Gospel of Mark." In *Voices from the Margin*, edited by R.S. Sugirtharajah, 85–104. London: ORBIS/SPCK, 1997.

Alciphron. *The Letters of Alciphron, Aelian and Philostratus.* Translated by Allen Rogers Benner and Francis H. Fobes. Cambridge: Harvard University Press, 1949.

Alexander of Aphrodisias. *De mixtione.* Translated by Robert B. Todd. Leiden: Brill, 1976.

Althusser, Louis. *Essays on Ideology.* London: Verso, 1984.

Anderson, Bernhard W. *From Creation to the New Creation: Old Testament Perspectives.* Minneapolis: Augsburg Fortress Press, 1994.

Arai, Jin. "Religious Education in 'Christ-with-Culture' from a Japanese Perspective." In *Religious Education* 91 (2) 1996: 222–37.

Aristides. *The Complete Works.* Vol. 2: *Orations XVII–LIII.* Edited by Charles A. P. Behr. Leiden: Brill, 1981.

Aristotle. Translated by Hugh Tredennick et al. 23 vols. Loeb Classical Library. Cambridge, Mass.: Harvard University Press, 1926–91.

Augustus. *Res Gestae Divi Augusti.* Translated by P. A. Brunt and J. M. Moore. London: Oxford University Press, 1967.

Baird, William. "One against the Other: Intra-Church Conflict in 1 Corinthians." In *The Conversation Continues: Studies in Paul and John,* edited by Robert Fortna and Beverly Gaventa, 116–36. Nashville: Abingdon, 1990.

Barclay, John M. G. "Neither Jew nor Greek: Multiculturalism and the New Perspective on Paul." In *Ethnicity and the Bible*, edited by Mark G. Brett, 197–214. Boston: Brill Publishers, 2002.

Barrett, C. K. *A Commentary on the First Epistle to the Corinthians.* New York: Harper & Row, 1968.

————. "Sectarian Diversity at Corinth." In *Paul and the Corinthians: Studies on a Community in Conflict,* edited by Trevor J. Burke and J. Keith Elliott, 287–302. Leiden: Brill, 2003.

Barth, Karl. *The Resurrection of the Dead.* Translated by H. J. Stenning. New York: Fleming H. Revell, 1933.

Barthes, Roland. "Theory of the Text." In *Untying the Text: A Post-Structuralist Reader,* edited by Robert Young, 31–49. Boston: Routledge & Kegan Paul, 1981.

Bassler, Jouette M. "1 Corinthians." In *Women's Bible Commentary*, edited by Carol Newsom and Sharon Ringe, 411–19. Louisville: Westminster/John Knox, 1998.

————. *Navigating Paul: An Introduction to Key Theological Concepts.* Louisville: Westminster/John Knox, 2007.

Baur, F. C. *Paul: His Life and Works.* Translated by E. Zeller. London: Williams and Norgate, 1873.

————. *The Church History of the First Three Centuries.* Translated by Allan Menzies. Vol.1. London: Williams and Norgatem, 1878.

Becker, Ernest. *The Denial of Death.* New York: Free Press, 1973.

Beker, J. C. *The Triumph of God: The Essence of Paul's Thought.* Minneapolis: Fortress Press, 1990.

Bellah, Robert N. *Habits of the Heart: Individualism and Commitment in American Life.* New York: Harper & Row, 1986.

Berger, Peter. *A Rumor of Angels.* Garden City, N.Y.: Doubleday, 1969.

————. *The Social Construction of Reality: A Treatise in the Sociology of Knowledge.* New York: Anchor Books, 1990.

————. *The Sacred Canopy: Elements of a Sociological Theory of Religion.* New York: Doubleday, 1967.

Berger, Peter, and Thomas Luckmann. *The Social Construction of Reality: A Treatise in the Sociology of Knowledge.* Garden City, N.Y.: Doubleday, 1967.

Betz, Hans Dieter, and Margaret Mitchell. "1 Corinthians." In *Anchor Bible Dictionary*. Vol. 1, edited by D. N. Freedman, 1139–48. New York: Double Day, 1992.

Bhabha, Homi. *The Location of Culture.* London and New York: Routledge, 1995.

Blount, Brian K. *Cultural Interpretation: Reorienting New Testament Criticism.* Minneapolis: Fortress Press, 1995.

Boers, Hendrikus. "The Meaning of Christ in Paul's Writings: A Structural-Semiotic Study." *Biblical Theology Bulletin* 14 (1984): 131–44.

Bonnell, Victoria E., and Lynn Hunt, eds. *Beyond the Cultural Turn: New Directions in the Study of Society and Culture.* Berkeley: University of California Press, 1999.

Bornkamm, Günter. *Paul.* Translated by D. M. G. Stalker. New York, Hagerstown, San Francisco, and London: Harper & Row, 1971.

Bourdieu, Pierre. *An Invitation to Reflexive Sociology.* Cambridge, U.K.: Polity, 1992.

Bousset, Wilhelm. *Kyrios and Christos.* Translated by John E. Steely. Nashville: Abingdon, 1970.

———. *What is Religion?* Translated by F. B. Low. New York and London: G. P. Putnam's Sons, 1907.

Bouttier, Michel. *En Christ: etude d'exegese et de theologie Pauliniennes.* Paris: Presses Universitaires de France, 1967.

Boyarin, Daniel. *A Radical Jew: Paul and the Politics of Identity.* Berkeley: University of California Press, 1994.

Braxton, Brad. *No Longer Slaves: Galatians and African American Experience.* Collegeville, Minn.: Liturgical, 2002.

———. *The Tyranny of Resolution: 1 Corinthians 7:17-24.* Atlanta: Society of Biblical Literature, 1999.

Brelsford, Theodore. "Christological Tensions in a Pluralistic Environment: Managing the Challenges of Fostering and Sustaining Both Identity and Openness." *Religious Education* 90, no. 2 (1995): 174–89.

Brett, Mark G. "Interpreting Ethnicity." In *Ethnicity and the Bible,* edited by Mark G. Brett, 3–22. Leiden and New York: Brill, 1996.

Brown, Alexandra R. *The Cross and Human Transformation: Paul's Apocalyptic Word in 1 Corinthians.* Minneapolis: Fortress Press, 1995.

Brown, Peter. *Society and Body: Men, Women, and Sexual Renunciation in Early Christianity.* New York: Columbia University Press, 1988.

Brueggemann, Walter. *Texts Under Negotiation: The Bible and Postmodern Imagination.* Minneapolis: Fortress Press, 1993.

Bultmann, Rudolf. *Kerygma and Myth.* Translated by Reginald H. Fuller. London, SPCK, 1962–64.

———. *Theology of the New Testament.* Vol.1, 2. Translated by Kendrick Grobel. New York: Charles Scribner's Sons, 1951.

———. *Faith and Understanding. Vol. 1.* Translated by Louise Pettibone Smith. London: SCM, 1969.

———. *The Presence of Eternity: History and Eschatology.* Westport, Conn.: Greenwood, 1975.

Burke, Trevor J. "Paul's Role as 'Father' to his Corinthian 'Children' in Socio-Historical Context (1 Corinthians 4:14-21)." In *Paul and the Corinthians: Studies on a Community in Conflict.* Edited by Trevor J. Burke and J. Keith Elliott, 95–113. Leiden: Brill, 2003.

Butting, Klara. "Pauline Variations on Genesis 2.24: Speaking of the Body of Christ in the Context of the Discussion of Lifestyles." *Journal for the Study of the New Testament* 79 (2000): 79–90.

Calvin. *First Epistle*. Translated by John Fraser. Edinburgh: Oliver and Boyd, 1960.

Caputo, John D. *Radical Hermeneutics: Repetition, Deconstruction, and the Hermeneutic Project*. Bloomington: Indiana University Press, 1987.

Castelli, Elizabeth. *Imitating Paul: A Discourse of Power*. Louisville: Westminster/John Knox, 1991.

Cerfaux, L. *The Church in the Theology of St. Paul*. New York: Herder, 1959.

Chariton. *Chaireas and Callirhoe*. Translated by G. P. Goold. Cambridge, Mass.: Harvard University Press, 1995.

Chong, Kelly H. "What It Means to Be Christian: The Role of Religion in the Construction of Ethnic Identity and Boundary among Second-Generation Korean Americans." *Sociology of Religion* 59, no. 3 (Fall 1998): 259–87.

Cicero. Translated by C. W. Keyes et al. 29 vols. Loeb Classical Library. Cambridge, Mass.: Harvard University Press, 1913–99.

Coakley, Sarah. "*Kenosis* and Subversion." In *Swallowing a Fishbone?* Edited by Daphne Hampson, 82–111. London: SPCK, 1996.

Collins, Raymond F. *First Corinthians*. Collegeville, Minn.: Liturgical, 1999.

Conzelmann, Hans. *1 Corinthians: A Commentary on the First Epistle to the Corinthians*, Hermeneia. Translated by James W. Leitch. Philadelphia: Fortress, 1975.

Cyprian. *The Letters of St. Cyprian of Carthage*. Translated by G. W. Clarke. New York: Newman, 1984.

Davies, Daniel M. "The Impact of Christianity upon Korea, 1884–1910: Six Key American and Korean Figures." *Journal of Church and State* 36 (1994): 795–820.

Davies, W. D. *Paul and Rabbinic Judaism: Some Rabbinic Elements in Pauline Theology*. 4th. ed. Philadelphia: Fortress Press, 1980.

Derrida, Jacques. "Différance." In *Margins of Philosophy*. Translated by Alan Bass. Chicago: The University of Chicago Press, 1982.

———. "Différance." In *Deconstruction and Context: Literature and Philosophy*. Edited by Mark C. Taylor, 396–420. Chicago: University of Chicago Press, 1986.

———. *Memoires: For Paul de Man*. Translated by Cecile Lindsay, Jonathan Culler, and Eduardo Cadava. New York: Columbia University Press, 1986.

———. *Negotiations: Interventions and Interviews, 1971–2001*. Edited, translated, and with an introduction by Elizabeth Rottenberg. Stanford: Stanford University Press, 2002.

———. *Of Grammatology*. Translated by Gayatri Chakravorty Spivak. Baltimore: Johns Hopkins University Press, 1974.

———. *Of Spirit: Heidegger and the Question*. Translated by Geoffrey Bennington and Rachel Bowlby. Chicago: University of Chicago Press, 1989.

———. "The Villanova Roundtable." In *Deconstruction in a Nutshell: A Conversation with Jacques Derrida.* Edited by John D. Caputo, 1–28. New York: Fordham University Press, 1997.

Diogenes Laertius. *Lives of Eminent Philosophers.* Translated by R. D. Hicks. 2 vols. Loeb Classical Library, Cambridge, Mass.: Harvard University Press, 1931–42.

Dio Chrysostom. Translated by H. Lamar Crosby et al. 5 vols. Loeb Classical Library, Cambridge, Mass.: Harvard University Press, 1932–51.

Dodd, C. H. *The Epistle of Paul to the Romans.* New York: R. Long & R. R. Smith, 1932.

Douglas, Mary. *Purity and Danger: An Analysis of the Concepts of Pollution and Taboo.* London and New York: Routledge, 2000.

Downing, F. Gerald. *Cynics, Paul and the Pauline Churches: Cynics and Christian Origins.* Vol. 2. London and New York: Routledge, 1998.

Dube, Musa W., and Jeffrey L. Staley, eds. *John and Postcolonialism: Travel, Space and Power.* London: Sheffield Academic Press, 2002.

Dunn, James. "'The Body of Christ' in Paul." In *Worship, Theology and Ministry in the Early Church: Essays in Honor of Ralph P. Martin,* edited by Michael J. Wilkins and Terence Paige, 146–62. JSNT Supp. 87.

———. *Jesus, Paul, and the Law: Studies in Mark and Galatians.* Louisville, Ky.: Westminster/John Knox, 1990.

———. *The Theology of Paul the Apostle.* Grand Rapids, Mich., and Cambridge, U.K.: Eerdmans, 1998.

Duran, Nicole Wilkinson, and Derya Demirer. "1 Corinthians 11 in Christian and Muslim Dialogue." In *Global Bible Commentary,* edited by Daniel Patte, 451–54. Nashville: Abingdon Press, 2004.

Durkheim, Emil. *The Division of Labor in Society.* Translated by George Simpson. New York: Free Press, 1933.

———. *The Elementary Forms of Religious Life.* Translated by Karen E. Fields. New York: Free Press, 1995.

———. *Montesquieu and Rousseau: Forerunners of Sociology.* Ann Arbor: University of Michigan Press, 1960.

Du Toit, Andrie. "'In Christ,' 'in the Spirit' and Related Prepositional Phrases: Their Relevance for a Discussion of Pauline Mysticism." In *Neotestamentica* 34, no. 2 (2000): 287–98.

Easthope, Anthony. *Literary into Cultural Studies.* London and New York: Routledge, 1991.

Ehrensperger, Kathy. "New Perspectives on Paul!—No New Perspectives on Romans in Feminist Theology?" In *Gender, Tradition and Romans: Shared Ground, Uncertain Borders,* edited by Cristina Grenholm and Daniel Patte, 227–55. London and New York: T&T Clark, 2005.

Elliott, John H., ed. "Patronage and Clientism in Early Christian Society." *Foundations and Facets Forum* 3, no.4 (Dec., 1987): 39–47.

Elliott, Neil. *Liberating Paul: The Justice of God and the Politics of the Apostle.* Maryknoll, N.Y.: Orbis Books, 1994.

———. "Paul's Letters: God's Justice against Empire." In *The New Testament—Introducing the Way of Discipleship,* edited by Wes Howard-Brook and Sharon H. Ringe, 122–47. Maryknoll, N.Y.: Orbis, 2002.

Ellis, E. Earle. "Christ Crucified." In *Reconciliation and Hope,* edited by Robert Banks, 69–75. Grand Rapids, Mich.: Eerdmans, 1974.

Fanon, Frantz. *Black Skin, White Masks.* Translated by Charles Lam Markmann. New York: Grove, 1967.

Fee, Gordon. *God's Empowering Presence: The Holy Spirit in the Letters of Paul.* Peabody, Mass.: Hendrickson, 1994.

———. "Toward a Theology of 1 Corinthians." In *Pauline Theology.* Vol. 2, edited by David M. Hay, 37–58. Minneapolis: Fortress Press, 1993.

Fiorenza, Elisabeth Schüssler. *In Memory of Her: A Feminist Theological Reconstruction of Christian Origins.* New York: Crossroad, 1983.

———. "Rhetorical Situation and Historical Reconstruction in 1 Corinthians." *New Testament Studies* 33 (1987): 386–403.

Furnish, Victor. "Belonging to Christ: A Paradigm for Ethics in First Corinthians." *Interpretation* 44 (1990): 145–57.

———. *Jesus According to Paul.* Cambridge, U.K.: Cambridge University Press, 1993.

———. "Theology in 1 Corinthians." In *Pauline Theology.* Vol. 2, edited by David M. Hay, 58–89. Minneapolis: Fortress Press, 1993.

———. *The Theology of the First Letter to the Corinthians.* Cambridge, U.K.: Cambridge University Press, 1999.

Gager, John G. "Body Symbols and Social Reality: Resurrection, Incarnation and Asceticism in Early Christianity." *Religion* 12 (1982): 345–63.

Garcia, Ricardo. *Teaching in a Pluralistic Society: Concepts, Models and Strategies.* New York: Harper & Row, 1982.

Gearon, Lian. "The Imagined Other: Postcolonial Theory and Religious Education." *British Journal of Religious Education* 23, no. 2 (2000): 98–106.

Grenholm, Cristina, and Daniel Patte. "Overture: Reception, Critical Interpretations, and Scriptural Criticism." In *Reading Israel in Romans: Legitimacy and Plausibility of Divergent Interpretations,* 1–54. Harrisburg, Pa: Trinity International Press, 2000.

Grosz, Elizabeth. *Space, Time, and Perversion.* New York: Routledge, 1995.

Gundry, Robert. *Soma in Biblical Theology with Emphasis on Pauline Anthropology,* 1–16. Cambridge: Cambridge University Press, 1976.

Gutiérrez, Gustavo. *On Job: God-Talk and the Suffering of the Innocent.* Translated by Matthew J. O'Connell. Maryknoll, N.Y.: Orbis, 1998.

Hampson, Daphne. "On Autonomy and Heteronomy." In *Swallowing a Fishbone?* edited by Daphne Hampson, 1–16. London: SPCK, 1996.

Hans, James S. *The Question of Value: Thinking through Nietzsche, Heidegger and Freud.* Carbondale: Southern Illinois University Press, 1989.

Hanson, K. C., and Douglas E. Oakman. *Palestine in the Time of Jesus: Social Structures and Social Conflicts.* Minneapolis: Fortress Press, 1998.

Harink, Douglas. *Paul among the Postliberals: Pauline Theology beyond Christendom and Modernity.* Grand Rapids, Mich.: Brazos, 2003.

Hengel, Martin. *Crucifixion.* Philadelphia: Fortress Press, 1977.

Heschel, Abraham J. *The Prophets: An Introduction.* Vol.1. New York: Harper Torchbooks, 1962.

———. *The Sabbath: Its Meaning for Modern Man.* New York: Farrar, Straus and Young, 1951.

Hiebert, Theodore, ed. *Toppling the Tower: Essays on Babel and Diversity.* Chicago: McCormick Theological Seminary, 2004.

Hollinger, Dennis P. *Individualism and Social Ethics.* Boston: University Press of America, 1983.

Hollingshead, James. *Household of Caesar and the Body of Christ: A Political Interpretation of the Letters from Paul.* Lanham: University Press of America, 1998.

Hooker, Morna. "Interchange in Christ and Ethics." *Journal for the Study of the New Testament* 25 (1985): 3–17.

hooks, bell. *Black Looks: Race and Representation.* Boston: South End, 1992.

———. *Yearning: Race, Gender, and Cultural Politics.* Boston: South End Press, 1990.

Horace. *Satires, Epistles, and Ars Poetica.* Translated by H. Fairclough. Loeb Classical Library. Cambridge, Mass.: Harvard University Press, 1970.

Horrell, David G. *The Social Ethos of the Corinthian Correspondence: Interests and Ideologies from 1 Corinthians to 1 Clement.* Edinburgh: T&T Clark, 1996.

Horsley, Richard. "1, 2 Corinthians." In *Postcolonial Biblical Criticism: Interdisciplinary Intersections,* edited by Stephen D. Moore and Fernando F. Segovia. Sheffield: Sheffield Academic, 2005.

———. *1 Corinthians.* Nashville: Abingdon, 1998.

———. "How Can Some of You Say that There Is No Resurrection of the Dead? Spiritual Elitism in Corinth." *Novum Testamentum* (1978): 203–31.

———. "Pneumatikos vs. Psychikos," *Harvard Theological Review* 69 (1976): 269–88.

———, ed. *Paul and Empire: Religion and Power in Roman Imperial Society.* Harrisburg: Trinity Press International, 1997.

———. *Paul and the Roman Imperial Order,* ed. Richard A. Horsley. Harrisburg, Pa.: Trinity Press International, 2004.

————. "Rhetoric and Empire—1 Corinthians." In *Paul and Politics: Ekklēsia, Israel, Imperium, Interpretation*, edited by Richard Horsley, 72–102. Harrisburg, Pa.: Trinity Press International, 2000.

Hutchison, William R. *Errand to the World: American Protestant Thought and Foreign Missions*. Chicago: University of Chicago Press, 1987.

Janssen, Claudia. "Bodily Resurrection (1 Cor 15)? The Discussion of the Resurrection in Karl Barth, Rudolf Bultmann, Dorothee Sölle and Contemporary Feminist Theology." *Journal for the Study of the New Testament* 79 (2000): 61–78.

Jeanrond, Werner G. "Love." In *The Oxford Companion to Christian Thought*, edited by Adrian Hastings, Alistair Mason, and Hugh Pyper, 395–97. Oxford: Oxford University Press, 2000.

Jewett, Robert. *Paul's Anthropological Terms: A Study of their Use in Conflict Settings*. Leiden: Brill, 1971.

————. *Paul the Apostle to America: Cultural Trends and Pauline Scholarship*. Louisville, Ky.: Westminster/John Knox, 1994.

————. "The Corruption and Redemption of Creation: Reading Romans 8:18-23 within the Imperial Context." In *Paul and the Roman Imperial Order,* edited by Richard Horsley, 25–46. Harrisburg, London, and New York: Trinity Press International, 2004.

Johnson, W. Stanley. "Christian Perfection as Love for God." In *Christian Ethics: An Inquiry into Christian Ethics from a Biblical Theological Perspective*, edited by Leon O. Hynson and Lane A. Scott, 97–113. Anderson, Ind.: Warner, 1983.

Josephus. *Jewish Antiquities*. Translated by St. J. Thackeray et al. 10 vols. Loeb Classical Library. Cambridge, Mass.: Harvard University Press, 1926–65.

Joubert, S. J. "Managing the Household: Paul as Paterfamilias of the Corinthian Household." In *Modeling Early Christianity: Social-Scientific Criticism of the New Testament in its Context*, edited by P. F. Esler, 213–23. London: Routledge, 1995.

Juvenal. *Satires*. Translated by Susanna Morton Braund. Cambridge, Mass.: Harvard University Press, 2004.

Käsemann, Ernst. *Exegetische Versuche und Besinnungen*. Vol. 1. Göttingen: Vandenhoeck and Ruprecht, 1960.

————. *Leib und Leib Christi: Eine Untersuchung zur Paulinischen Begrifflichkeit*. Tübingen: Mohr, 1933.

————. *Perspectives on Paul*. Translated by Margaret Kohl. Philadelphia: Fortress Press, 1971.

Keck, Leander. "Paul as Thinker." *Interpretation* 47 (1993): 27–38.

Kim, Yung Suk. "Jesus' Death in Context." *The Living Pulpit* 16, no. 2 (2007).

————. "Korea, South, Christianity in." In *Cambridge Dictionary of Christianity*. Cambridge: Cambridge University Press, forthcoming.

King, Ursula. "Feminist Theologies in Contemporary Contexts: A Provisional Assessment." In *Is There a Future for Feminist Theology?* Edited by Deborah Sawyer and Diane Collier. Sheffield: Sheffield Academic, 1999.

Kingsbury, Jack. *Matthew as Story*. Philadelphia: Fortress, 1988.

Klauck, Hans-Josef. *The Religious Context of Early Christianity.* Translated by Brian McNeil. Edinburgh: T&T Clark, 2000.

Knight, Douglas. "Ethics and Human Life in the Hebrew Bible." In *Justice and the Holy,* edited by Douglas A. Knight and Peter J. Paris, 65–88. Atlanta: Scholars Press, 1989.

Kwok, Pui Lan, "Discovering the Bible in the Non-biblical World." In *Voices from the Margin*, edited by R. S. Sugirtharajah, 289–305. Maryknoll, N.Y.: Orbis, 1997.

Lee, Jung Young. *Marginality: The Key to Multicultural Theology*. Minneapolis: Fortress, 1995.

Lee, Michelle. *Paul, the Stoics, and the Body of Christ*: Cambridge: Cambridge University Press, 2006.

Lefebvre, Henri. *The Production of Space.* Translated by Donald Nicholson-Smith. Oxford: Blackwell, 1991.

Levenson, Jon D. "The Universal Horizon of Biblical Particularism." In *Ethnicity and the Bible*, edited by Mark G. Brett, 143–69. Boston: Brill, 2002.

Liddell, Henry G. *Greek English Lexicon*. New York: Oxford University Press, 1996.

Lightfoot, J. B. *Notes on the Epistles of Paul*. Grand Rapids, Mich.: Baker, 1980.

Livy. *History of Rome.* Translated by B. O. Foster et al. 14 vols. Loeb Classical Library. Cambridge, Mass.: Harvard University Press, 1919–59.

Lowe, Walter. *Theology and Difference: The Wound of Reason.* Indianapolis: Indiana University Press, 1993.

Malina, Bruce, and Richard Rohrbaugh. *Commentary on the Synoptic Gospels.* Minneapolis: Fortress Press, 2003.

Manilius. *Astronomica*. Translated by G. P. Goold. Loeb Classical Library. Cambridge, Mass.: Harvard University Press, 1977.

Martin, Dale. *The Corinthian Body*. New Haven: Yale University Press, 1995.

McLaren, Margaret A. *Feminism, Foucault, and Embodied Subjectivity.* New York: SUNY Press, 2002.

Meeks, Wayne. *The First Urban Christians: The Social World of the Apostle Paul.* New Haven: Yale University Press, 1983.

Merriam, Charles E. *Political Power, Its Composition and Incidence*. New York and London: McGraw-Hill, 1934.

Metz, Johann Baptist. *Faith in History and Society: Toward a Practical Fundamental Theology.* Translated by David Smith. New York: Seabury, 1980.

Minear, P. S. *Images of the Church in the New Testament*. Philadelphia: Westminster, 1961.

Minh-ha, Trinh T. "Cotton and Iron." In *Out There: Marginalization and Contemporary Cultures,* edited by Russel Ferguson, Martha Gever, Trinh T. Minh-ha, and Cornel West, 327–36. New York: M.I.T. Press, 1990.

Mitchell, Margaret. *Paul and the Rhetoric of Reconciliation. An Exegetical Investigation of the Language and Composition of 1 Corinthians.* Louisville, Ky.: Westminster/John Knox, 1992.

Munt, Sally R. "Framing Intelligibility, Identity, and Selfhood: A Reconstruction of Spatio-Temporal Models." In "Auto/bio/geography: Considering Space and Identity." Special issue, *Reconstruction* 2, no. 3 (Summer 2002), http://reconstruction.eserver.org/023/munt.htm.

Myers, Ched. "Balancing Abundance and Need." *The Other Side* 34, no.5 (1998): 14–19.

Nasuti, Harry. "The Woes of the Prophets and the Rights of the Apostle: The Internal Dynamics of 1 Corinthians 9." *Catholic Biblical Quarterly* 50 (1988): 246–64.

Neugerbauer, Fritz. "Das Paulinische 'in Christo.'" *New Testament Studies* 4 (1957–58): 124–38.

Neyrey, Jerome. *Paul, in Other Words: A Cultural Reading of His Letters.* Louisville, Ky.: Westminster/John Knox, 1990.

Nygren, Andres. *Agape and Eros.* Part 1. Translated by A. G. Herbert. London and New York: Macmillan, 1932.

———. *Christ and His Church.* Translated by Alan Carlsten. Philadelphia: Westminster, 1956.

O'Conner-Murphy, Jerome. "1 Corinthians 11:2-16 Once Again." *Catholic Biblical Quarterly* 50 (1988): 265–74.

Odell-Scott, David. "Editor's Dilema." *Biblical Theology Bulletin* 30 no. 2 (2000): 68–74.

———. "In Defense of an Egalitarian Interpretation of First Corinthians 14:34-36: A Reply to Murphy-O'Connor's Critique," *Biblical Theology Bulletin* 17, no. 3 (1987): 68–74.

———. "Let the Women Speak in Church: An Egalitarian Interpretation of First Corinthians 14:33b-36." *Biblical Theology Bulletin* 13, no. 3 (1983): 90–93.

———. *Paul's Critique of Theocracy: A/Theocracy in Corinthians and Galatians.* London and New York: T&T Clark International, 2003.

Papanikolaou, Aristotle. "Person, *Kenosis* and Abuse: Hans Urs von Balthasar and Feminist Theologies in Conversation." *Modern Theology* 19 (2003): 41–65.

Pathrapankal, Joseph. "1 Corinthians." In the *Global Bible Commentary,* 444–50. Nashville: Abingdon, 2004.

Patte, Daniel. "Can One Be Critical without Being Autobiographical? The Case of Romans 1:26-27." In *Autobiographical Biblical Criticism: Academic*

Border Crossings—A Hermeneutical Challenge, edited by Ingrid Rosa Kitszberger. Leiden: Deo Publishing, 2003.

———. *The Gospel According to Matthew: A Structural Commentary on Matthew's Faith*. Philadelphia: Fortress Press, 1987.

———. *Paul's Faith and the Power of the Gospel: A Structural Introduction to the Pauline Letters*. Philadelphia: Fortress Press, 1983.

———. *The Religious Dimensions of Biblical Texts: Greimas's Structural Semiotics and Biblical Exegesis*. Semeia Studies. Atlanta: Scholars, 1990.

———. *Structural Exegesis for New Testament Critics*. Guide for Biblical Scholarship. Minneapolis: Fortress Press, 1990.

Philo. Translated by F. H. Colson and G. H. Whitaker. 12 vols. Loeb Classical Library. Cambridge, Mass.: Harvard University Press, 1929–62.

Philodemus. De Pietate. Translated by Dirk Obbink. New York: Oxford University Press, 1997.

Plato. Translated by H. N. Fowler. 12 vols. Cambridge, Mass.: Harvard University Press, 1914–39.

Plautus. Translated by Paul Nixon. Cambridge, Mass.: Harvard University Press; London: W. Heinemann, 1950–52.

Plutarch. *Conjugalia Praecepta*. Translated by Sarah B. Pomeroy. New York: Oxford University Press, 1999.

Polaski, Sandra H. *Paul and the Discourse of Power*. Sheffield: Sheffield Academic, 1999.

Ramsaran, Rollin A. "Resisting Imperial Domination and Influence: Paul's Apocalyptic Rhetoric in 1 Corinthians." In *Paul and the Roman Imperial Order*, 89–101. Harrisburg, PA: Trinity Press International, 2004.

Ricoeur, Paul. *Oneself as Another*. Translated by Kathleen Blamey. Chicago and London: University of Chicago Press, 1992.

———. *The Rule of the Metaphor: Multi-disciplinary Studies in the Creation of Meaning in Language*. Translated by R. Czerny. London: Routledge & Kegan Paul. 1978.

———. *Time and Narrative*. Vol. 3. Chicago: University of Chicago Press, 1988.

Robertson, C. K. *Conflict in Corinth: Redefining the System*. New York: P. Lang, 2001.

Robinson, J. A. T. *The Body: A Study in Pauline Theology*. London: SCM, 1952.

Robinson, Wheeler. *Corporate Personality in Ancient Israel*. Philadelphia: Fortress Press, 1980.

Saldarini, Anthony J. *Matthew's Christian-Jewish Community*. Chicago: University of Chicago Press, 1994.

———. *Pharisees, Scribes and Sadducees in Palestinian Society: A Sociological Approach*. Wilmington, Del.: M. Glazier, 1988.

Sampley, Paul. "1 Corinthians." In *New Interpreter's Study Bible*, 2047. Nashville: Abingdon, 2003.

Sanders, Boykin. "1 Corinthians." In *True to Our Native Land,* edited by Brian Blount, 276–306. Minneapolis: Fortress, 2007.

Schmithals, W. *Gnosticism in Corinth. An Investigation of the Letters to the Corinthians.* Nashville: Abingdon, 1971.

Schweitzer, Albert. *The Mysticism of Paul the Apostle.* Translated by William Montgomery. New York: Henry Holt & Co., 1931.

Schweizer, Eduardo. *The Church as the Body of Christ.* Richmond: John Knox Press, 1964.

———. "The Church as the Missionary Body of Christ." *New Testament Studies* 8 (1961): 5.

———. "soma *ktl.*" In *Theological Dictionary of the New Testament* 7 (1971): 1074–80.

———. "soma." *Theological Dictionary of the New Testament* 7: 1064.

Segovia, Fernando F. *Decolonizing Biblical Studies: A View from the Margins.* New York: Orbis, 2000.

———. "'And They Began to Speak in Other Tongues': Competing Modes of Discourse in Contemporary Biblical Criticism." In *Reading from this Place.* Vol. 1, edited by F. F. Segovia and M. A. Tolbert. Minneapolis: Fortress Press, 1995.

Segovia, Fernando F. and Mary Ann Tolbert, eds. *Reading from this Place.* Vol.1, 2. Minneapolis: Fortress, 1995.

Seneca. Translated by Richard M. Gummere. 10 vols. Loeb Classical Library. Cambridge, Mass.: Harvard University Press, 1917–72.

Setzer, Claudia. "Resurrection of the Dead as Symbol and Strategy," *Journal of the American Academy of Religion* 69, no. 1 (2001): 65–95.

*Sextus Empiricus.*Translated by R. G. Bury. 4 vols. Loeb Classical Library. Cambridge, Mass.: Harvard University Press, 1933–49.

Sibley, David. *Geographies of Exclusion.* London: Routledge, 1995.

Sobrino, Jon. *Christ the Liberator: A View from the Victims.* Translated by Paul Burns. Maryknoll, N.Y.: Orbis, 2001.

Sölle, Dorothee. "Der Mensch zwischen Geist und Materie: warum und in welchem Sinne muss die Theologie materialistisch sein?" In *Der Gott der kleinen Leute: sozialgeschichtliche Bibelauslegungen, Bd 2: Neues Testament,* edited by Willy Schottroff and Wolfgang Stegemann, 15–36. Munich: Christian Kaiser, 1979.

Stendhal, Krister. "The Apostle Paul and the Introspective Conscience of the West." *Harvard Theological Review* 56 (1963): 199–215.

———. "Religious Pluralism and the Claim to Uniqueness." In *Education as Transformation:Religious Pluralism, Spirituality, and a New Vision for Higher Education in America,* edited by Victor H. Kazanjian Jr. and Peter L. Laurence, 181–83. New York: Peter Lang, 2000.

Stowers, Stanley. *A Rereading of Romans: Justice, Jews, and Gentiles.* New Haven: Yale University Press, 1997.

Strecker, Georg. *Theology of the New Testament.* Translated by Eugene Boring. Louisville: Wesminster/John Knox, 2000.

Sugirtharajah. R. S., ed. *Voices from the Margin: Interpreting the Bible in the Third World.* London: ORBIS/SPCK, 1997.

Tacitus. *Annales.* Translated by Alfred John Church and William Jackson Brodribb. New York: Modern Library, 2003.

Tan Yak-Hwee. "Judging and Community in Romans: An Action within the Boundaries." In *Gender, Tradition and Romans: Shared Ground, Uncertain Borders,* edited by Cristina Grenholm and Daniel Patte, 39–62. T&T Clark, 2005.

Taylor, Mark Kline. *Remembering Esperanza: A Cultural-Political Theology for North American Praxis.* Maryknoll, N.Y.: Orbis, 1990.

Theissen, Gerd. *The Social Setting of Pauline Christianity: Essays on Corinth.* Translated by John H. Schütz. Philadelphia: Fortress, 1982.

———. *Sociology of Early Palestinian Christianity.* Translated by John Bowden. Philadelphia: Fortress, 1978.

Thompson, John B. *Ideology and Modern Culture: Critical Social Theory in the Era of Mass Communication.* Stanford: Stanford University Press, 1990.

Troeltsch, Ernst. *The Absoluteness of Christianity and the History of Religions.* Translated by David Reid. Richmond: John Knox, 1971.

Trompf, Garry W. "On Attitudes toward Women in Paul and Paulinist Literature: 1 Corinthians 11:3-16 and its Context." *Catholic Biblical Quarterly* 42 (1980): 196–215.

Turner, Bryan. *The Body and Society: Explorations in Social Theory.* 2nd ed. London and Thousand Oaks, Calif.: Sage Publications, 1996.

Varro. *Lingua Latina.* Translated by Roland G. Kent. Cambridge, Mass.: Harvard University Press, 1932.

Wainwright, Elaine. *Toward a Feminist Critical Reading of the Gospel according to Matthew.* Berlin and New York: Walter de Gruyter, 1991.

———. "A Voice from the Margin: Reading Matthew 15:21-28 in an Australian Feminist Key." In *Reading from This Place.* Vol. 2, 132–53. Minneapolis: Fortress, 1995.

Walker, William. O. "1 Corinthians and Paul's Views Regarding Women." *Journal Biblical Literature* 94 (1974): 94–110.

Wanamaker, Charles. "A Rhetoric of Power: Ideology and 1 Corinthians 1–4." In *Paul and the Corinthians: Studies on a Community in Conflict,* edited by Trevor J. Burke and J. Keith Elliott. Leiden: Brill, 2003.

Warrior, Robert. "A Native American Perspective: Canaanites, Cowboys, and Indians." In *Voices from the Margin: Interpreting the Bible in the Third*

World, edited by R. S. Sugirtharajah, 287–95. Maryknoll, N.Y.: Orbis, 1991.

Wedderburn, A. J. M. "Some Observations on Paul's Use of the Phrases 'in Christ' and 'with Christ.'" *Journal for the Study of the New Testament* 25 (1985): 83–97.

——. "The Body of Christ and Related Concepts in 1 Corinthians," *Scottish Journal of Theology* 24 (1971): 74–96.

Welborn, Laurence L. *Paul, the Fool of Christ: A Study of 1 Corinthians 1–4 in the Cosmic-Philosophic Tradition*. London and New York: T&T Clark International, 2005.

Wilder, Amos. "Eschatological Imagery and Earthly Circumstance." *New Testament Studies* 5 (1958–59): 229–45.

Williams, Barclay B. *Christ in You: A Study in Paul's Theology and Ethics*. Lanham, Md.: University Press of America, 1999.

Willis, Wendell. "An Apostolic Apology? The Form and Function of 1 Corinthians 9." *Journal for the Study of the New Testament* 24 (1985): 33–48.

Wire, Antoinette Clark. *The Corinthian Women Prophets: A Reconstruction through Paul's Rhetoric*. Minneapolis: Fortress, 1990.

Witherington, Ben. *Conflict and Community in Corinth: A Socio-Rhetorical Commentary on 1 and 2 Corinthians*. Grand Rapids: W. B. Eerdmans, 1995.

Yagi, Seiichi. "*I* in the Words of Jesus." In *Voices from the Margins*, 330–51. London: SPCK, 1991.

Index

PAUL IN CRITICAL CONTEXTS

Other Titles in the Series

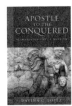

Apostle to the Conquered

Reimagining Paul's Mission

Davina C. Lopez

ISBN 978-0-8006-6281-3

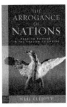

The Arrogance of Nations

Reading Romans in the Shadow of Empire

Neil Elliott

ISBN 978-0-8006-3844-3

Galatians Re-Imagined

Reading with the Eyes of the Vanquished

Brigitte Kahl

ISBN 978-0-8006-3864-1

Onesimus Our Brother

Reading Religion, Race, and Slavery in Philemon

Matthew V. Johnson, James A. Noel, and Demetrius K. Williams, eds.

ISBN 978-0-8006-6341-4

The Politics of Heaven

Women, Gender, and Empire in the Study of Paul

Joseph A. Marchal

ISBN 978-0-8006-6300-1

call 800-328-4648

fortresspress.com